THE
HUMAN SIDE
OF
SUCCESSFUL
COMMUNICATION

By Robert E. Moore

THE
HUMAN SIDE
OF
SUCCESSFUL
COMMUNICATION

PRENTICE-HALL, INC., ENGLEWOOD CLIFFS, N.J.

OTHER BOOKS BY ROBERT E. MOORE

Man Alive

The Human Side of Selling

Automation in Business Communication

Turn On the Green Lights in Your Life

Let's Not Worry, Let's Not Fuss!

On-the-Job Communication Workshop
(a workshop seminar for business people)

DEDICATION

This book is dedicated to the
Family Service Association of America
in appreciation of the FSAA members
throughout the United States and Canada
whose counseling helps more than 300,000
families each year talk out their problems
and arrive at a better understanding.

ACKNOWLEDGMENTS

The many case histories in this book are reports of the experiences of men and women who told me about their problems in communicating with others at home or at work. I appreciate their cooperation. Where it was desirable, I have changed names to avoid identifying a physician or to avoid embarrassing his patients, the members of a family or an employee's boss. Without the information given me by physicians, psychologists, clergymen and men and women in many different occupations, it would not have been possible to discuss so many specific problems in interpersonal communications and analyze the most effective ways to solve them. I acknowledge the generous, and often enthusiastic, cooperation from the many who answered my question: "Do you ever feel that it is difficult to get others to listen to you and understand you?"

Particularly I thank Al Taylor of Family Service Association of America for reading the manuscript and his associates and staff for making case histories and other material available to me. I am grateful to the following for giving me permission to quote: Dr. Gerald Gordon, Chief—Psychiatric Section, E. I. Du Pont de Nemours & Company; Lawrence A. Appley, President and Fred Schneider, Membership Director American Management Association; S. Rains Wallace, Jr., Director of Research of the Life Insurance Agency Association; C. E. Duggan, Director of Service, National Sales Executives, Inc.; Louis Wozar, President of The Tait Manufacturing Company, and several publishers. I acknowledge the reports of research projects, surveys and other material supplied by the public relations department of the University of Michigan and the information on this subject received from Yale, Princeton, Northwestern and California Universities.

"All of us ask ourselves almost daily, 'How can we achieve better communications?' I hear it constantly, at meetings, on the lecture platform, at industry gatherings. The need for better communications is one of the most profound needs of our time —yet few take the time to do anything about it.

ARTHUR B. LANGLIE, PRESIDENT MC CALL CORP.

WHY THIS BOOK WILL INTEREST YOU

If you and I were astronauts and were approaching the planet Mars in the first successful space ship, I'm sure I would listen carefully to every word you spoke. Our interests would be the same—to land that space ship safely on Mars. So we would listen to each other.

There would be few outside influences to distract us. No pressure of other duties to pull our attention away, no conflict of interest. We'd be all alone in the cockpit of a ship zooming through space towards a mysterious planet.

Whenever either of us spoke, the chances are his communication would get immediate and complete attention. Each would concentrate on understanding the other's words. Each would be predisposed to react as the other wanted him to. Our communications would be successful.

In our every day contacts with others with whom we live and work, we seldom get such concentrated attention. There are so many things that distract those around us. And everyone seems so preoccupied with matters of great concern to himself. Often it is difficult to get another person to really listen and understand us.

As Arthur Langlie emphasized, the need for better communications is one of the most profound needs of our time. What are we doing about it?

In the field of electronic communications, billions are being spent for improvements. Frederick R. Kappel, President of American Telephone and Telegraph Company, said recently that the Bell System alone will spend 2½ billion dollars for new equipment and new services in one year.

He said, "We bounced telephone calls off the moon and Echo I, as a prelude to a world-wide satellite communication system."

And he also said, "We developed Data-Phone service so that electronic business machines can 'talk' to each other over regular telephone lines." He added, "Some day machines will do more talking than people!"

When machines do more talking than people perhaps they will understand each other automatically. This does not happen when one person talks to another. Getting another to understand, or even listen, isn't easy.

How can we communicate more successfully?

Most experts tell us that there are two essentials for effective interpersonal communication: (1) you must express yourself clearly and (2) the other person must listen.

When John talks to Mary, John must express himself in words that Mary can understand, and Mary must listen if she is to understand what John has to say.

But suppose Mary doesn't want to listen, isn't interested in John or in what John is saying. No one can make her listen to John or try to understand John no matter how clearly he expresses himself.

My observations have shown that there is a third factor which is the key essential for the success of interpersonal communications:

Mary must want to listen to John—the
other person must *want to listen*
to what you have to say.

In this book we will discuss the reasons why some of those with whom we live and work may not want to listen when we talk to them, and we will determine what we can do to make them *want* to listen and understand us.

ROBERT EMMET MOORE

TABLE OF CONTENTS

PART I

HOW TO GET OTHERS TO LISTEN TO US AND UNDERSTAND US

Chapter 1

Chapter 2

Chapter 3

15

PART II

SUCCESSFUL COMMUNICATION IN YOUR HOME

Chapter 9

PART III

SUCCESSFUL COMMUNICATION AT WORK

Chapter 10

Chapter 11

Chapter 12

CONCLUSION

THE
HUMAN SIDE
OF
SUCCESSFUL
COMMUNICATION

HOW TO GET OTHERS TO LISTEN
AND UNDERSTAND US

"We are all in a desert.
Nobody understands anybody."

GUSTAVE FLAUBERT

Chapter 1

WHY ISN'T IT ALWAYS EASY
TO GET OTHERS TO LISTEN
AND UNDERSTAND US?

Have you ever had the feeling, when you were talking
to someone, that he didn't understand you, perhaps wasn't even
listening to you? Could you tell by the far-away look in his
eyes that his mind was wandering? Or did he interrupt you
from time to time and seem more anxious to tell you what he
was thinking than to hear what you wanted to say?

If you feel that it is difficult, at least on some occasions, to
get others to listen to you and understand you, you have a lot
of company.

*Evidently everyone has trouble at times
getting others to understand him*

For some time I have been asking people of many different
types—from housewives to corporation executives, from clerks
in retail stores to clergymen—"Do you have any trouble getting
others to understand you?" Without exception every one has
answered, "Yes!"

When I've asked, "Why is this so?" I've heard many sug-

23

gested reasons from, "People are so busy with their own thoughts," to, "There are a lot of jerks in the world." Many have told me of frustrating experiences they have had trying to communicate with other people.

Her fiancé wasn't listening

For instance, a school teacher said, "I was talking to my fiancé last night about some things that happened at school during the day. After a while he started to look out the window and I suspected he wasn't listening to me. So I said, 'Harold!' He didn't answer. I said, 'Harold, you aren't listening to me!' He shook his head as if he was clearing his mind and said, 'I'm sorry, my mind was far away.' I knew he hadn't heard a word I said."

When I asked a lawyer whether he had any trouble getting people to understand him, he said, "I certainly do. Doesn't everybody?"

He added, "Sometimes when I come home in the evening I say to my wife, 'I'm beginning to think the world is full of idiots!' Fortunately, my wife is one person who usually understands me. She just lets me alone for fifteen or twenty minutes while I have a couple of highballs. Then I'm fit to live with. It takes a lot out of a person trying to make others understand what he is trying to say these days."

Is it safe to assume that others understand us?

Perhaps it is natural for us to assume that because we know what we're talking about, the people who listen to us should understand us. But do they? Even members of our own families sometimes do not understand what we say to them. A husband said, "I told my wife the taxes on our home were going to be increased and I explained the reason for this. Later the same evening she asked, 'Did you say we are going to be clobbered with another tax increase?' She knew I had said something about taxes, but she probably hadn't heard or understood a word I said!"

It seems that getting our thoughts through to others is not an easy task. This is true in business as well as at home. A team of University of Michigan psychologists found evidence of many communication failures among the top-level business-men they studied.

Even when two people work closely together they sometimes do not understand each other

The psychologists interviewed key men in a number of manufacturing, oil, and utility companies and they found that the boss seldom knew what his junior executive's problems were. Frequently the two men did not even agree on what the subordinate was supposed to be doing!

Only 6 per cent understood each other completely

In only 6 per cent of the cases were the two men in complete agreement about the junior executive's problems. In 20 per cent of the cases there was some agreement. In 74 per cent of the cases there was practically no agreement about the areas of trouble.

Isn't this rather amazing evidence of communication failure among management people whose positions would indicate that they are above average in intelligence and education!

$112,000,000 to improve communications

The need for more successful communication in business is enormous. The American Management Association estimates that industry is spending over $112,000,000 a year on publications designed to help employees improve their ability to communicate with each other.

Yes, the need to improve communication in business is urgent, almost as urgent as it is in many homes.

Are nine out of ten divorces caused by communication failure?

During a recent lecture I estimated that nine out of ten divorces were caused by a breakdown in communications between husband and wife. Some of the people in the audience seemed to be surprised by this estimate. They probably were thinking of the reasons usually given for divorce—disagreements over finances, sex, in-laws, perhaps incompatibility, or so-called cruel and inhuman treatment. But what are most of these but breakdowns in communications between two people? A man and a woman who had hoped to spend their lives together reach the point where they can't tolerate each other. Every discussion they have seems to end in disagreement, hurt feelings, bitterness.

A marriage counselor, who has helped many couples try to save their marriages, said, "The inability of husband and wife to communicate with each other successfully is the big problem in marriages today."

How frequently do communications break down in the home?

Perhaps few of us realize just how frequently a communication breakdown occurs in our homes. Consider the fact that there are some 800,000 divorces a year. More than 10,000,000 Americans have been divorced at least once—one out of every nine adults.

Do men leave home because they can't talk over their troubles with their wives?

It is reported that almost 1,000,000 men desert their wives and disappear each year. When one thoughtless word leads to another, the husband and wife probably refuse to listen to each other's side of their disagreements. They don't try to understand each other and the marriage cracks up.

According to the Family Service Association of America, whose members help thousands of disturbed husbands and wives understand each other, the clash between two married people often is due to complete lack of communication!

Are many suicides caused by a breakdown in communication?

In his book, *Man Against Himself,** Karl A. Menninger tells us that someone kills himself in the United States every 24 minutes, 60 times a day, 22,000 times a year.

Dr. Menninger said, "This is only in the United States; it is twice as frequent in some European countries. It is everywhere more frequent than murder." Why do some people take their own lives? No one knows definitely. It is my belief that many suicides are the result of failure on the human side of communication.

Perhaps these unfortunate people feel, as Gustave Flaubert suggested, that they are alone in a desert—nobody understands them. It is possible that they were hurt deeply by communication mistakes such as those we discuss in the next chapter.

Wouldn't it be wonderful if better understanding of the human side of successful communication could prevent tragedies of this sort!

Why isn't it always easy to communicate successfully?

First of all, let us define "successful communication." When we communicate successfully with another person we do three things: (1) we get him to listen to us, (2) understand us, and (3) react to what we say as we want him to.

When we accomplish all three, we communicate successfully. Sometimes this is easy. Often, however, it is extremely difficult. The problems involved in transferring our thoughts to the minds of other people are so great, an army of psychologists,

---

* Published by Harcourt, Brace & World, Inc., New York.

sociologists, semanticists, and other experts are studying inter-personal communication today. Their findings make us aware of the fact that there are many reasons why other people may not be eager to listen to us or to understand what we say.

For instance, no other person ever thinks about all life's problems and challenges exactly as you do. Why? Because no one has exactly the same frame of reference that you have. Your frame of reference includes your point of view, your education, your inherited traits, your environment, your entire background.

As you know, no two people ever have exactly the same hereditary traits and environment. Even in the same family, brother and sister may be miles apart in temperament because there are so many variations in the possible combination of genes. The genes are the determiners of hereditary traits. According to one authority, there are almost three hundred trillion possible combinations of genes that can take place from the union of a human egg and sperm. So how can two individuals ever be exactly the same?

Each of us is a distinctive individual. We live and work with other distinctive individuals. We must communicate with them. Therefore, we must know what obstacles we must overcome to transmit our thoughts to the minds of other people.

Four areas of stress that make communication difficult

An analysis of the factors which determine the success of communication at home or at work reveal four areas of stress which seem to be the principal causes of communication breakdown today. They are:

1. The constant bombardment of words.
2. The 4 to 1 speed ratio of mind and tongue.
3. The reliance on effective expression which does not necessarily enable one to make an effective "impression" on the mind of another.

4. The decisive stress—failure on the human side of communications.

How the constant bombardment of words makes communication difficult

In the popular Broadway musical *My Fair Lady*, Eliza Doolittle shrieks, "Words! Words! Words! I'm so sick of words!" Eliza expresses the feelings of millions of other people.

Professor Richard Meier, social scientist in the University of Michigan Mental Health Research Institute, said, "There are perils involved in the unlimited growth of communications. The transmission of messages of all kinds is increasing steadily. Communications are interactions between human beings. As the quantity of interactions increase, we feel that some kind of limit exists. At some point, probably different for each person, he becomes harassed by too many messages; the pace of communications becomes stressful."

The pressure of too many words can become irritating

Professor Meier added, "When the pressure becomes intense many of us try to escape. In the simpler systems of nature, the lemmings march to their destruction in the sea due to a state of shock induced from interacting with other lemmings." Professor Meier cited research findings with rats and rabbits that tend to support this belief.

When a person becomes harassed by the many messages he receives from people with whom he comes in contact all day, plus the telephone, the radio, television, the postman, the newspapers and magazines, the educational system, community organizers, the office or factory bulletins, reports and memos, he is much less willing to listen attentively to what you have to say. He becomes irritated more easily. He is much more inclined to tune you out.

It is so easy for others to tune us out

If you are familiar with television sales, you know that the remote control has become quite popular. Why? A neighbor who bought a new TV set just because he wanted the remote control calls the control a "blab-off." He said, "We use our blab-off constantly to shut out annoying commercials or to tune out unpleasant programs." No doubt, many of those with whom we try to communicate use a mental "blab-off." They tune us out when we annoy them or do not interest them.

This can happen often today when those whose attention we try to get are harassed by so many messages from so many different sources. This is one of the reasons it is not easy to get others to listen to us and understand us.

*How the 4 to 1 speed ratio of mind and tongue
make it difficult for your listener to concentrate
on what you are saying*

When Professor Ralph G. Nichols of the University of Minnesota was addressing an Industrial Relations Conference at the University of Michigan, he said, "The average person speaks at the rate of 125 words per minute among his family and friends, 100 words per minute in front of an audience. But most of us think at a 'cruising speed' of 400 to 500 words per minute.

"As a result of this," Professor Nichols said, "most of us have trouble holding the other person's attention."

When you consider that the person with whom you are talking can think four or five times as rapidly as you speak, you become aware of the fact that you must have something interesting to say to him or you will lose him.

If you will imagine the driver of an automobile speeding across a desert at 100 to 125 miles an hour trying to keep in touch with a jet plane cruising overhead at 400 to 500 miles an hour, you will have some idea of the reason it is so difficult to get another person to keep his mind in contact with yours while you are speaking to him.

If the driver of the automobile contacted the pilot of the plane by radio telephone, he might say, "Hello there! I'm testing my new Jaguar. Isn't it a beauty? Look how fast I'm going —a hundred and twenty-five miles an hour. I think she'll do more. I'm a darn good driver and I want to see how fast my new car will go." Before he finished expressing his thoughts the plane would be out of sight. Unless the pilot happened to be interested in the driver of the automobile, he, no doubt, would simply turn a knob on his radio phone and quickly tune out this one-sided attempt at communication.

How can we tell when another's mind is cruising far away? By the blank look in his eyes. By the way he interrupts. By the lack of interest he shows. In many ways the other person lets us know we've lost him. And we can lose our listener easily unless we cultivate skill in using the techniques that help us succeed on the human side of communication.

Our reliance on effective "expression" can lead us to assume we are communicating successfully when we are not

All through school we are taught to express ourselves properly. Most of us can. It is important, of course, to choose the right words to express our thoughts and it is necessary to follow the rules of grammar, at least within reason.

If you have any questions about your vocabulary or your grammar, read one of the many good books on grammar or vocabulary building or take one of the courses (day or night) in English or effective speaking.

The truth about vocabulary building

We all know a person who builds a larger vocabulary can express himself more effectively. However, there is a difference between "expressing" yourself and "impressing" your thoughts on the mind of another person.

For instance, Fred Clark, a salesman, was boasting to a friend about how smart his sister is. He said, "Ever since she went away to college she's been learning ten new words a day. She uses the new words in the letters she writes me. This has been going on now for more than a year."

The friend said, "Say, at ten words a day she learns three thousand six hundred and fifty new words a year! She must write interesting letters."

Fred said, "She used to. But now I can't understand half of what she says unless I look up the new words in a dictionary."

If you think that story unusual, consider the results of a survey the Air Force made to determine why Air Force directives were hard to understand. It was found that Air Force writing was difficult to understand because it required a reading skill equivalent to that of a senior in college.

The survey showed 93 per cent of the airmen had no college education and only 32 per cent of the officers were college graduates. Obviously, therefore, a communication which required the reading skill of a college senior would not be readily understood by many of the airmen and some of the officers.

We must choose words our listeners understand

A large vocabulary does make it possible for you to express yourself in many more ways than the person who understands only a limited number of words. However, the truth about vocabulary building is this: don't assume that it gives you the key to other people's minds. It doesn't.

As the Air Force survey suggests, there is a vast difference between "expressing" ourselves well and "impressing" our thoughts in the minds of other people.

*One of the "secrets" of Winston Churchill's success
in communicating with other people*

A friend who said he listened to every one of Winston
Churchill's speeches he possibly could told me he thinks some
of Churchill's greatness is due to his simple language. This
friend said, "He never used a four-syllable word if a one- or two-
syllable word would do."

Mr. Churchill's promise to the English people during World
War II probably will be a highlight in history down through the
ages. You remember his words—"Blood, toil, tears and sweat!"

You didn't have to be at any particular education level to
understand those words.

Some communication experts believe that too much emphasis
is placed on "verbal mechanics." In the popular book *Language,
Meaning and Maturity,** Professor Wendell Johnson of the
State University of Iowa said, "It appears that teachers of
English teach English so poorly largely because they teach
grammar so well. . . . The teacher of English appears to attempt
to place the emphasis upon writing rather than upon writing-
about-something-for-someone."

It is natural for an English teacher to emphasize the rules
for writing or speaking correctly. And these rules are important.
Unquestionably, they help us express ourselves more effectively. However, we must remember that our objective in
speaking to another person is not only to express ourselves, but
to make an "impression" on his mind. As Professor Wendell
Johnson pointed out, we make an impression on others only
when we write or talk "about something for the someone" with
whom we wish to communicate.

*The decisive factor—the human side of
successful communication*

One of the principal reasons for communication failure is

---

* *Language, Meaning and Maturity,* edited by S. I. Hayakawa. Harper &
Brothers, New York.

that many of us have assumed that because other people have ears they would or should listen to us and understand us. We expect them to adjust to our viewpoint. This they seldom are willing to do.

When we found that others didn't understand us, we might think, "They're just jerks!" Or we might say, as the lawyer to whom I referred earlier in this chapter said, "The world is full of idiots!" We explain our failure to communicate successfully by blaming others for not listening carefully.

Perhaps they don't want to listen

If others don't listen to us and understand us, perhaps the reason is they aren't interested in what we have to say, so they don't *want* to listen. Probably, they don't *want* to listen because we haven't taken into account the human side of successful communication. People are not insensitive I.B.M. machines that react automatically when a message is fed into them.

Failure on the human side of communications may cause hurt, resentment, annoyance, boredom. If a person with whom we would communicate doesn't like what we say or how we say it, he shuts us out with his mental "blab-off." He may appear to be listening, but his thoughts can cruise far away in areas that interest him.

How to make others want to listen to whatever we have to say

There is a comparatively simple technique which can make your communications more successful. This is based on an awareness of the other person and his interests. The technique is rather easy to learn. If you are not now using it, I suggest you try it.

In one sense, it is as easy as learning your ABC's. You need only remember the successful human side techniques and use them. This may not be easy if you have to replace old habits of

self-centered thinking with new and active interest in everyone you meet. But this can be one of your most rewarding
experiences.

Here, in essence, is the human side of communications in
simple ABC form:

A. Study the other person—learn to sense his needs and his
   reactions.
B. Communicate with him in terms of his own interest.
C. Show your interest in him.

If we don't try to understand the person with whom we wish
to communicate, we can't very well sense his needs or probable
reactions to what we intend to say. So we may not even try to
talk or write in terms of his interest. Often we merely "express" ourselves, discuss our own interests. Consequently our
words may never register in the illusive mind we try to reach.
Furthermore we can make some serious mistakes that alienate
other people and cause them to lose interest in anything we
have to say.

Sometimes we "put our foot in our mouth"

In the next chapter we will discuss some of the mistakes many
of us make on the human side of communications. These mistakes repel the listener. Probably we seldom make these mistakes deliberately. We make them "without thinking." And this
is bad! However, a few minutes of self-appraisal may show us
where we have been "putting our foot in our mouth" and
causing a breakdown in communications between ourselves
and those with whom we live and work.

When we recognize our own mistakes, we can avoid them in
the future. If we avoid them, we will see an immediate improvement in our ability to communicate successfully.

In the third chapter we will discuss the techniques for
achieving success on the human side of communications. In
succeeding chapters we will explore some of the ways in which

we can apply these techniques in specific circumstances that will improve our communications at home and at work.

Let us remember as we go through this book together that the other person's mind is his own private domain. He lets us in only when he understands us and *when we interest him.*

He will understand us and we will interest him when we use the techniques that make us successful on the human side of communications.

"Mend your speech a little, lest it may mar your fortunes."

WILLIAM SHAKESPEARE

Chapter **2**

HOW WOULD YOU RATE YOUR ABILITY
TO MAKE OTHERS WANT TO LISTEN
AND UNDERSTAND YOU?

The subject of a first session of a Communication Work-shop program I developed for business organizations is "How Successfully Are We Communicating Now?"

One evening recently I joined a group of executives of a well-known corporation to discuss this question. Before the meeting the leader of the group turned to me and said he didn't believe the discussion would last long. He said, "I don't think it will take an hour to decide how well we're communicating now. I think we're doing pretty well. This will be a short session."

Two hours later, after listening to the workshop participants exchange ideas about the many areas in which they thought communications could be improved, he turned to me and asked, "How can we stop this discussion? It could continue all night!"

The men and women around the table seemed glad to have an opportunity to tell what was unsatisfactory about some of the communications between individuals and between departments and they suggested ways these could be made more effective.

Each one of these executives has a manual two or three inches thick in which every step of the organization's procedure is explained in detail. The instructions on how to communicate with each other are clear. The breakdowns discussed were not in inter-department routines. They were on "the human side" of the communications.

Most of the complaints were about thoughtlessness or carelessness of other people. Some individuals were too abrupt in their communications. Some assumed the other person knew more than he actually did and were sarcastic. Some were critical. Some were just cold and showed no interest in the other person.

How successfully are you communicating with the members of your family?

If you called a conference of the members of your family this evening and asked them to discuss the question, "How successfully are we communicating with each other?" what complaints and what suggestions do you think you would hear?

Perhaps the members of most families assume they are communicating effectively just as the officers of many business organizations do. As one executive told me, "We frequently are too close to the situation to realize just what is happening. We are inclined to assume that because we are rocking along pretty well our communication practices are satisfactory. But this is not necessarily so, as we have found."

Any of us may be making mistakes in communicating with others he doesn't realize he's making. We think we're expressing ourselves effectively, but at times others do not respond the way we want them to. They seldom tell us why. Perhaps they simply do not understand us and don't care to try. Even in our own families our mistakes can narrow the range of our communications to the point where we just discuss the same old things every day—eating and sleeping and routine household matters. Some of us may be in much the same position Pierre found himself in.

Pierre couldn't speak one word of English when he came to this country to visit a friend. However, the friend accompanied him on sightseeing trips and on visits to mutual acquaintances so it wasn't necessary for Pierre to speak English. One day, however, he told his friend that he would like to be able to go to a restaurant and order something in English just for the experience. He said, "Isn't there something that every restaurant has that I can ask for?"

His friend said, "Yes there is. Every restaurant is sure to have apple pie and coffee. You will be safe therefore to go into any restaurant, regardless of size, and ask the waiter or waitress for apple pie and coffee."

Pierre practiced saying "apple pie and coffee" for hours. After a day or two he had enough confidence in himself to go to a restaurant alone. He sat at the counter and asked the waitress for "apple pie and coffee." It sounded to the waitress like "opple pie and coffee," but she understood him well enough to bring him what he ordered. Pierre was delighted. Day after day he went to restaurants and ordered "apple pie and coffee." His communication was adequate. He always got apple pie and coffee.

In a few weeks, however, he tired of apple pie and coffee. He asked his friend, "Is there something else that every restaurant has that I could order?"

His friend said, "Why yes, every restaurant serves ham sandwiches. You'll be safe if you ask for a ham sandwich."

Pierre practiced saying "ham sandwich," until he was confident he could say this clearly. Then he went to a restaurant, sat at the counter and smiled as the waitress came toward him. She asked, "What will you have?" Confidently, he said, "Ham sandwich!"

The waitress asked, "White or rye?"

Pierre looked startled for an instant. A blank expression

crossed his face. Then he smiled sheepishly and said, "Apple pie and coffee."

Many of us probably never know the questions in other peoples' minds as we try to communicate with them. Perhaps it doesn't occur to us to wonder what they might think. Consequently, we don't succeed in making them understand us. Therefore, we may go through a good part of our lives settling for monotonous "apple pie and coffee" when we could also have all the "ham sandwiches" we want if we knew how to make ourselves understood.

The other person translates everything we say into terms of his own experience, his own interests

Psychologists tell us it is seldom that anything we say means exactly the same thing to another person as it does to us. The other person translates everything we say into terms of his own experience and his own interests. He rarely adjusts his thinking to our point of view.

In some cases another person may not even try to understand us, because we have closed his mind through any one of dozens of communication blunders we may have made.

When our attitude and our words show the other person that we aren't particularly interested in him, or when we hurt his feelings, he often withdraws behind a barrier of belligerent or bored indifference.

You can't say to your wife, "You should have looked in the mirror before you bought those tight slacks!" or "What do you do with all the money I give you?" and expect her to like it. You can't say to your husband, "If you're so smart, you take over raising the children." Or "Why aren't you as successful as my sister's husband?" and not expect him to resent it.

Once a person has become resentful or indifferent he can be as hard to communicate with successfully as the most cold blooded of the diplomats who pound their fists on the table at the United Nations.

When you hurt another person's feelings you're in trouble

Some of us learn at an early age that communication mistakes can be painful. For instance, thoughtless words have given many a boy a black eye.

When a small boy comes home with his first black eye, his mother usually asks, "How did you get that?" Perhaps the boy says, "He started it!"

When the mother asks, "How did he start it?" the boy might answer, "He said his dad was better than my dad because he's vice president of a bank. And he said his dad could lick mine! I told him he was a big fat liar and he got mad and hit me. I hit him back though, and he's got a black eye, too. I guess he won't be getting smart with me any more!"

Both of these boys evidently understood the "mechanics" of communication. There was nothing wrong with their sentence structure or their syntax. However, neither was aware of the importance of "the human side." Each hurt the other's feelings, made him resentful and angry.

Junior was right—after that argument the other boy "will not get smart" with him again. In fact, he probably will not be interested in communicating with Junior or in listening to anything Junior has to say. The thoughtless remarks we make to others may not produce a black eye. However, they can make even those who love us much less interested in listening to us and trying to understand us.

Furthermore, inconsiderate remarks have an accumulative effect. They pile up resentment and can turn a person's mind away from us long after we've forgotten what we did or said that hurt his feelings. For instance, several days after a foreman criticized one of his men in front of the man's fellow workers, the foreman called a meeting to discuss a new management program for reducing waste. The man who had been criticized publicly said to another man sitting next to him in the meeting room, "I'm not interested in anything that louse says. He can't tell me a thing, the big loud mouth."

Have you any bad communication habits?

Without realizing it, you may have developed the habit of making serious mistakes on the human side of your communications. You never would make them again if you were aware of the way they keep you from transferring your thoughts successfully to other peoples' minds.

We have listed a number of the mistakes often made in the home and at work. All the possible errors in communications are not listed by any means. However, enough are given to enable you to appraise yourself. In the privacy of your own study, go over this list. Ask yourself, "Do I really do this or say that?"

After you have checked the entire list, how would you rate your ability to communicate successfully? How many of these communication mistakes do you make? And how frequently? If you are making any of the mistakes listed, try to avoid them in the future. Why close other peoples' minds to your ideas?

Do you make any of these mistakes in communicating with others at home or at work?

At Home   *Often   Seldom   Never*

1. Do you talk about yourself, your experiences, your ideas, every chance you get? ....

2. Do you become impatient or angry when others do not agree with you? ....

3. Do you interrupt others and change the subject to one that interests you? ....

4. Do you criticize your mate's handling of money? ....

At Home   *Often   Seldom   Never*

5. Are you sarcastic? ....

6. Do you nag? ....

7. Do you complain about your health, your weight, your problems whenever anyone appears to be listening? ....

8. Do you make fun of others' (a) ideas (b) friends (c) clothes? ....

9. Do you boast about all you do for the family? ....

10. Do you read or walk away while others talk to you? ....

11. Do you argue instead of discussing differences of opinion? ....

12. Do you rebuke one member of your family before the others? ....

13. Do you insist on having your way even if it inconveniences the rest of the family? ....

14. Do you lose your temper? ....

15. Do you raise your voice and shout at others when you're angry? ....

16. Do you ridicule members of your family? ....

17. Do you try to monopolize the conversation? ....

18. Do you talk repeatedly about your "good old days"? ....

At Home	Often	Seldom	Never
19. Are you quick to contradict others in your family?			
20. Do you discuss your family troubles at social gatherings?			
21. Do you talk about your worries, about ill health or any other unpleasant subject at the dinner table?			
22. Do you show that you are suspicious of the motives of others in your family?			
23. Do you walk around your home with a chip on your shoulder and take every criticism as a personal affront?			
24. Do you order your children to do things instead of asking them to?			
25. Do you insist on making decisions for your children?			

At Work	Often	Seldom	Never
1. Do you quarrel with fellow workers?			
2. Do you listen impatiently when someone tells you his opinion?			
3. Do you show that your feelings are hurt if you are asked to change something you've done?			
4. Do you try to force your opinions on others?			

At Work   *Often   Seldom   Never*

5. Do you make sarcastic remarks about others or their work? ....

6. Do you reprimand one person in the presence of others? ....

7. Do you argue for the right to do things your way? ....

8. Do you lose your temper? ....

9. Are you a complainer—the "cry baby" of your organization? ....

10. Do you usually find fault with others' plans? ....

11. Do you become a grouch at times? ....

12. Do you make promises you don't intend to keep? ....

13. When you become angry, do you shout at others across the office, the store, or the shop? ....

14. Do you use profanity when you get into an argument? ....

15. Do you give the impression that you are more important than others because (a) you've been there longer? (b) you have a better position? ....

16. Do you show you're not interested in considering new ideas about your job? ....

17. Do you kick up a fuss or sulk when someone offers constructive criticism? ....

At Work	*Often*	*Seldom*	*Never*
18. Are you belligerent when you talk to your boss as though you're talking to an enemy?			
19. Do you discuss your personal problems with co-workers?			
20. Do you criticize your fellow workers, your supervisor and the organization that employs you?			
21. If you work in a store, do you look bored when a customer comes in and you have to serve him?			
22. Do you argue with customers?			
23. Do you try to force your own opinion on customers?			
24. Do you become impatient and tell customers they are wrong?			
25. Do you keep on arranging stock or making entries in a sales book without even looking up when you know a customer is waiting for your attention?			

There are many ways in which we can communicate the fact that we are interested only in ourselves and not in those with whom we live and work. When we do this, we build resentment and make people unwilling to listen to us and to try to understand us.

When people don't *want* to listen to you or understand you, no one in the world can make them!

Thoughtless communication mistakes
can wreck a happy home

Marriage counselors say that many husbands and wives barely talk to each other. Why? Perhaps because one or the other has made some of the mistakes we've just discussed. They've hurt each other's feelings and aren't interested in listening or trying to understand. Any chance for companionship or a true understanding of each other has gone out the window. They live on a monotonous word diet of "apple pie and coffee" when an awareness of the power of the human side of communications could help them get all the "ham sandwiches" they would ever want.

Self-centered communications nearly
ruined this business

In business organizations communication mistakes such as those we listed can make it very unpleasant for people to work together. If these mistakes become widespread, they can ruin an organization. When Louis Wozar became manager of the Dayton Pump and Manufacturing Company, the owner, Frank M. Tait, was ready to close the business and release its 250 employees. It had been losing money for some time. Louis Wozar found conditions so bad that various members of management were not speaking to each other. Even though they shared the same office they communicated only through terse notes sent back and forth by messenger.

Wozar changed this situation quickly. He had the office desks repositioned, set up improved channels of communication, called group meetings and individual conferences with department heads, supervisors, and individual workmen. He soon won their confidence and stimulated their enthusiasm. In a short time, the company (which has since been renamed Tait Manufacturing Company) began to prosper and it has now regained its position of leadership in its field.

How successfully are you communicating now at home, at work?

What is happening in your home, in your place of business? Are you on a restricted "apple pie and coffee" routine because various individuals aren't really listening or trying to understand each other? What can you do to make them *want* to listen to you, understand you and cooperate in making your home life and work successful?

The human side of communication technique can help you, if you will use it. We'll discuss the ways to use it in the next chapter.

"*The manner in which one single ray of light, one single precious hint will clarify and energize the whole mental life of him who receives it, is among the most wonderful and heavenly of intellectual phenomena.*"

ARNOLD BENNETT

Chapter **3**

HOW TO IMPROVE THE HUMAN SIDE
OF OUR COMMUNICATION

While discussing the human side of successful communications with a friend the other evening he said, "I have been married twice, as you know. If I had realized before I married my first wife that she was so self-centered, I would never have married her. Don't misunderstand me. I'm not criticizing this girl. She was a very fine person, but interested only in herself. Her mind revolved around the first person singular—I, me, mine. This I couldn't cope with. So we broke up in a year or so."

"Was the fault entirely hers?" I asked.

"No," he said. "I was just as much to blame. As I said, I couldn't cope with the situation. If I knew as much about the human side of communications as I know now, I think I might have been able to handle it."

I said, "Your present marriage to Laura seems to be quite successful."

"Yes it is," he said. "As you know, we've been married fifteen years. We're as different as two people could be. We have our disagreements certainly. However, when we have a disagreement usually we try to find what solution is best for the two of us. Neither tries to impose his opinion on the other or argue just to prove he is right. This is unusual I find. Particularly is it unusual in business."

"What do you mean?" I asked.

His boss reminds him of his first wife

He said, "I work for a boss who has many of the characteristics of my first wife. He's a complete egocentric. For instance, after a conference today I asked him what he thought of the opinions expressed by other department heads. He said, 'Their views were pretty much the same as mine. However, I thought I summarized the problem pretty well. I think these conferences are a waste of time, but I guess I have to give the boys a chance to express themselves. As you know, I usually have to make all the important decisions myself.' Notice how often he used 'I.'

"He's the head of our outfit and evidently he needs to have his importance recognized. But, on second thought, I guess this is a general need. Perhaps he isn't so much of an exception after all."

My friend was expressing his understanding of an important factor in the human side of communication. He realizes that egocentric people are not exceptions. We must learn how to communicate with them.

Usually we talk about things
from our own viewpoint

Most of us are interested primarily in ourselves. This is one of the reasons we don't communicate successfully at times. Each of us talks about a subject from his own point of view—in terms of his own interests. If the other person isn't particularly interested, often he doesn't listen or try to understand. Or he might tell us where we're wrong and insist on explaining his opinion.

This could provoke an argument and make it difficult to communicate successfully.

How to make others want to listen to us and understand us

We can't force another person to listen to us and understand us. We must make him *want* to do this. How can we make someone *want* to listen to us and try to understand us? By using this ABC technique for successful communications. The ABC's of success on the human side are:

A. Study the other person—learn to sense his needs and his reactions.
B. Communicate with him in terms of his own interests.
C. Show your interest in him.

Study the other person

To communicate successfully with another person we must get him to put out of his mind whatever is in it when we start to speak. We must get him to slow down his thinking to the speed of 100 to 125 words a minute at which we talk. We must get him to listen with an open mind. We begin our study of him therefore by asking ourselves, "What is going on in his mind most of the time?"

My observations have shown that we can find a good part of the answer to this question by determining on which of three levels of maturity the other person happens to be. If you will analyze the people you see every day at home or at work, you will find that each one is an "I-Lander," a "We-Lander," or on rare occasions a "You-Lander."

No doubt there are many ways to measure maturity. To me a person's maturity can be determined by his ability and willingness to get along with others.

Recognize the first level of maturity

The first level of maturity is that of the I-Lander. The thinking of a person on this popular plateau revolves around the pronoun used most frequently throughout the world—the first person singular, "I." He thinks in terms of I want, I insist, I think, I believe, I'm right, I'm interested, or I'm not interested—almost invariably "I" or "Me" or "Mine."

The I-Lander knows he has to live and work with others, but he isn't particularly interested in other people unless they can do something for him, unless they agree with him, amuse him, or please him.

We call this first type of person an I-Lander because he lives in the land of "I," behind a barricade of indifference to anything outside of his own personal interest.

What are his interests? His own security, his success, his property, his power, his reputation, his taste, his affections, his sentiment, his amusement, his experience. In other words, himself.

The manager of the trust department in a large New York bank congratulated one of his stenographers on her forthcoming marriage. He said, "You must be very happy to have found the man you want."

She replied, "Yes I am. Now I won't have to work any more. I'll have a home of my own. My mother won't be able to tell me what to do. If I want to sleep late, I'll be able to sleep as long as I want to. I've found the man I want who can give me the things I want." She evidently thought in terms of "I want," always "I."

This is typical I-Lander thinking. A young man who was asked why he intended to get married said, "I want companionship. I want someone to love me. I want someone to cook for me. I want a home. I want children. I want someone to take care of my home and children." Again, "I want"—"I"—"I"—"I"—"I."

Most of us are I-Landers

As you study the people you meet, you probably will decide that most of them are I-Landers.

Show almost anyone a photograph of his class at school or a business dinner he attended. What is the first thing he does? He looks for his own picture. Then he might say, "Here I am! I didn't take a very good picture, did I? Guess I was blinking my eyes when the photographer snapped this picture."

If you happen to be in the group that was photographed, he seldom looks for you. So you ask him to let you see the photo and start looking for the most important person of all—yourself. Most of us are I-Landers, interested primarily in ourselves.

In our study of those with whom we want to communicate it is well to consider that everyone is an I-Lander until we find evidence that he is on a higher level of maturity. To get I-Landers to listen to us and understand us, we must penetrate their indifference to anything but themselves.

Of course some I-Landers are more intelligent than others. The intelligent ones realize they have to deal with fellow I-Landers so they treat them as brothers in the fraternity of "I."

Cultivating the ability to recognize the I-Landers of the world, and learning how to communicate successfully with them, has made many men and women successful at home and in business.

The We-Landers

The second level of maturity is the level of the We-Landers. Usually not more than one out of ten of the people we meet will be a We-Lander. A We-Lander thinks in terms of "we." He is interested in "what is good for us."

For instance, contrast the thinking of Jane and Sarah. Jane confided to a friend that she keeps a bank account her husband doesn't know she has. If she buys something on a charge account, decides to return it to the store and gets cash for it, she puts this cash in her own private account. She considers this money that she didn't expect to have. To her it is "found" money and therefore rightfully hers.

When she works part time, as she does occasionally, she puts the money into her own account. She said she would never pay any household expenses with her own money. It is hers to spend. After all, she says, it is her husband's obligation to support her. She insists, "Any money that I earn or that I save or get from any source is mine."

Jane and Sarah are both college graduates. Both are charming girls. They just happen to think differently. At a party just before Sarah's marriage, one of her friends said, "You've been working for ten or eleven years for your company and you must have quite a bit of money coming in your pension retirement fund. Think of the fun you're going to have spending all that money on yourself. What clothes you can buy!" Sarah replied, "That money isn't mine any more. After tomorrow when Jim and I are married, it will be Jim's and mine." This was said without any fanfare. It was just a simple statement of Sarah's attitude.

Sarah has been married more than ten years and her marriage is unusually successful. Jim evidently has no trouble communicating with her. She is a We-Lander. A We-Lander thinks in terms of "we" and "our"—"What is best for us?" A We-Lander is predisposed to listen to you and to find something mutually beneficial in whatever you have to say. You seldom have a problem communicating with a We-Lander.

The You-Landers

This is the highest level of maturity. It is attained by most of us only at rare enlightened intervals.

You have no communication problems with this rare individual because you know that he is interested in assisting you in becoming more successful in everything you undertake.

Wonderful world of I-Landers

As you study more and more people, you realize that this is a world of I-Landers. Most of us are pretty much interested in ourselves and the things we want. Is this bad? Of course, we'd have Utopia if we were all You-Landers or at least We-Landers. But, let's face it, this is an I-Lander world. For instance, telephone company surveys show that the word most frequently used in telephone conversations is "I." However, this need not disturb us. It can be a wonderful world if we recognize the primary interest of most of those around us and learn how to communicate with them successfully.

What interests him now?

In addition to determining the level of maturity of the persons with whom we wish to communicate, it is necessary that we learn what happens to interest him at the time we approach him. This is essential because we want to communicate with him in terms of his own interest.

People may think alike in a general way, but we know that no two think exactly alike. No two have exactly the same background. Few have exactly the same interests at any given time. No matter how close we are to the other person, therefore, we must not assume that we know what he is thinking at the time we are talking to him. We must find out so we can communicate successfully.

The lesson of the choir and the crickets

One summer evening two elderly sisters were sitting in their rocking chairs on the front porch of their little home on the edge of a village in Vermont. As they rocked back and forth one of the sisters was listening to the choir practicing in the little church down the road to her left. The choir was singing one of her favorite songs. Looking down the road where she could see the light shining through the stained glass windows of the little church, she said to her sister, "Isn't that the sweetest music you ever heard in your life?"

Her sister, who was sitting at her right, happened to be looking toward the fields on her side of the house. She was listening to the crickets chirping in the twilight. As she rocked back and forth she smiled happily and said, "Yes, that is beautiful music and I've heard that they do it by rubbing their hind legs together."

Here we have an example of the difference between expressing yourself and making the impression you want in the mind of another person. We see that it is not enough to "express" yourself correctly. There was nothing wrong with the way the first sister expressed herself. Her words were simple and clear. Her sentence structure was good. There were no split infinitives, nor did she end a sentence with a dangling preposition. Yet her own sister did not understand her. Why? Because her sister's mind was soaring off in another direction. She was thinking of something that interested her at the moment.

How can we tell what another person is thinking at any time? By asking questions to determine the interest of the other person.

If the first sister had asked, "Are you listening to the choir practicing down the street?" she would have learned what was in her sister's mind immediately. Then if she had listened to the crickets for a minute and had said, "I listen to them every evening, too. I love to hear them. But just now I have been listening to the choir down the road. They're singing one of our favorite hymns. Can you hear them?" When the other answered, "Yes," the first sister would know they were thinking about the same thing. Therefore, when she said, "Isn't that the most beautiful music you've ever heard?" her sister would have understood her.

When we study the person with whom we want to communicate in order to sense his needs and his reactions, we first determine his probable level of maturity and his interests at the time we approach him. Then we are ready for the second step in the ABC technique for achieving success on the human side of communication.

Communicate with others in terms of their own interests

Because most of us are I-Landers, too, it is difficult for us to communicate with others in terms of their own interests. We are much more inclined to talk about what concerns us. Take the case of a father who was worried about the grades of his nine-year-old son in reading and writing. The father told a doctor friend, "I don't know what to do with Billy. His teachers say he has a high I.Q. and he learns easily. But he just won't study reading and writing. He says he wants to be an automobile mechanic when he grows up and not a writer or a teacher. He says he can pick up enough reading and writing without studying."

The doctor asked, "What have you been doing to get him to study?"

The father said, "I've chewed him out about this plenty. I've raised hell with him, but it hasn't done any good. I tried cutting out his allowance. I've kept him away from TV. I've made him sit at the table with his books in front of him. But nothing has done any good. He just won't study."

The doctor suggested, "Send him in to see me. I'll have a talk with him."

When Billy came to the office, the doctor said, "I understand you don't want to drive a car."

Billy asked, "What do you mean I don't want to drive a car?"

The doctor said, "Well, your father tells me you aren't studying reading and writing."

Billy asked, "What does that have to do with driving a car?"

The doctor said, "Why, you know you have to take an examination before you can get a driver's license, don't you?"

The boy said, "Sure, but what has that got to do with reading and writing?"

"Well, first of all," the doctor said, "you have to read all the traffic laws in the state in which you apply for your license. You must learn all the safety regulations. Then you must take a written test to prove that you have read these laws and regulations and understand them. This you must do in Connecticut before they even let you take the driver's test."

Billy looked surprised, but he said, "Aw, I can learn enough about that stuff to get by I guess."

"But how are you going to repair your car or even change spark plugs if you can't read and write?" the doctor asked.

"What has changing spark plugs got to do with reading and writing?" Billy wanted to know.

The doctor said, "You've got to be able to read an instruction manual to learn how to set the gap in your spark plugs properly. If the gap is too wide, your engine balks when you're going up a steep hill. If it's too narrow, the engine heats up rapidly. So you open your instruction manual and find that you have to set the gap in the spark plugs a certain width, say, 0.35, so you take out your little gadget and measure 0.35 and then set your spark plugs so your engine functions properly."

Billy scratched his head. He said, "Gee, I didn't know that."

The doctor said, "Think it over, Billy." Billy did. A few months later his father told the doctor that Billy was studying conscientiously and he was getting A's in reading and writing. Why was the family physician able to do what the father couldn't do? He talked to Billy in terms of his own interest.

When we talk to others in terms of their own interests they want to listen to us and they try to understand us. When they try, they usually do.

What is the principal interest of the person with whom you want to communicate? If he's an I-Lander, you know he is interested in himself and in everything else in terms of how it affects him. Knowing this, you slant your communications accordingly. When you do, he is much more likely to keep his mind from wandering away when you talk to him.

Talk in terms of the other person's interests and he'll *want* to listen to what you have to say.

Show your interest in the other person

In chapter one we defined the term "successful communication." You remember that we pointed out that to communicate successfully with another person we must accomplish three things: 1) get him to listen to us, 2) understand us, and 3) react favorably to what we say. If you watch the effect you have on others when you talk to them, you'll find that they are much more inclined to react favorably, that is, as you want them to, when you show that you are interested in them.

The key step in the ABC technique for success on the human side of communication is this one—*show others that you are interested in them.*

How do you do this? Of course you avoid the irritating mistakes we discussed in chapter two. We don't irritate a person in whom we really are interested. In addition, however, you demonstrate your interest in the other person in each of the following ways:

1. Through your recognition
2. Through your attention
3. Through the tone of your voice
4. Through your actions
5. Through your appearance

How recognition demonstrates interest

If, when another person walks into the room, you look up with a frown, and your attitude indicates that you are thinking, "Oh, it's you again!" or "Go away. Don't bother me!" the other person will put up his I-Lander defenses and it will be difficult for you to communicate successfully with him. If, on the other hand, you smile warmly and show that you are glad to see him, he will be much more likely to listen favorably to anything you have to say.

A very successful mother of a young girl uses an expression of recognition which I recommend to everyone who wants to communicate more successfully. When her daughter comes downstairs in the morning, the mother says, "Look who's here!" She says this as though a princess has just walked into the room. The daughter holds her head up proudly. She is an important person. She is recognized!

Does she listen when her mother speaks? She surely does. And does she react to her mother's suggestions as the mother wants her to? She certainly does. Is she willing to wash the dishes, take care of the baby, or do anything else her mother asks her to do? You bet she is. She listens favorably to any suggestions her mother makes.

Make people feel important

It isn't necessary to say, "Look who's here!" whenever someone walks into the room—but *think this way*. Let the other person see by your expression that you're glad to see him, that you think he's important. Each one is important to himself, you know, and he will be more inclined to listen favorably to you when he sees you, too, recognize him as an important individual.

Greet people by name

When showing your recognition for another person, greet him by name. Use his name from time to time during your conversation. All of us love the sound of our names. What else is so closely identified with each of us?

A friend told me that he complained to his wife that the whole family seemed to have forgotten his name. He said, "The children call me 'dad.' You sometimes call me 'dad' or 'darling.' The only time I hear my name around here is when a visitor drops in to see us."

His wife said, "But you are the children's 'dad.' And I thought you liked that name. When I call you 'darling' or 'dear' I'm using a term of endearment. I should think you'd like this."

He said, "Oh, I like it all right. But have you ever stopped to think that those terms could apply to any other father or husband in town? Every father is a 'dad' and every husband is his wife's 'darling' or 'dear.' You'll think I'm silly, but I do like to hear my name occasionally and I bet you do, too!"

His wife agreed. "You're right, Tom. I love to hear you call me 'Nancy.' I'll remember that and you won't be just 'dad' or 'darling' any more. You'll be 'Tom' to me."

Few men would ask their families to call them by name as Tom did. Who would ever ask his business associates to greet him by name? Yet there seems to be a deep need for this recognition. When we give this to another person we demonstrate our interest in him and he is much more inclined to listen to what we have to say.

How your attention shows your interest

To demonstrate your interest in another person it is essential that you give him your complete attention while he is speaking. Much has been written about the necessity for "listening" to the other person. To some people listening means merely not talking. This is not enough. If we want the other person to be attentive when we speak to him, we must give him our complete attention whenever he speaks to us.

In some homes the wife will be running a vacuum cleaner while her husband talks to her and she'll say, "Go right ahead, dear, I'm listening to you." He might ask, "How can you hear me with that thing making so much noise?" She might reply, "Well I have to clean this rug, you know. Go ahead, I can hear you."

How you listen tells whether you are really interested in the other person

Probably she does listen. However, her husband knows it

isn't possible for a person to give his complete attention to two things at one time. He feels she considers whatever he has to say not important enough to turn off the vacuum cleaner and listen. This actually is what she is telling him—that she isn't interested enough to stop and listen attentively.

In a store a sales clerk might continue to check stock or write in his sales book while a customer is talking to him. In an office one person may go through his mail while another is talking. In each case, the "busy" person might say, "Go right ahead, I'm listening." He intends to listen. But something in the sales slip or in the stock he is checking or in the mail he is sorting attracts his attention and he loses the gist of what the other person is saying. But, more important, his lack of attention tells the other person, "I'm not particularly interested in you." Being human, the other's natural reaction is to think, "If you're not interested in me, I'm not interested in anything you might have to say."

It is essential, as you can see, that we give those with whom we wish to communicate our complete attention when they are talking to us. In this way we show them again that we are interested in them. Usually they become more interested in us.

How the tone of your voice reveals your interest

The tone of our voice often tells the listener more than our words do.

If you have a dog, you can see the importance of the tone of your voice in communication by making this simple test. Call your dog in an angry tone as though you're going to punish him. Even though you say: "Come here!" he may hide behind a chair or cringe in a corner afraid to come to you.

Now say the same words in a cheerful voice, as though you're going to pat him. Immediately his expression changes. His tail wags. He comes running confidently to you.

Your voice reflects the way you feel toward each person you meet. To get others to listen willingly and consider favorably what you have to say, be sure your voice sounds pleasant and suggests a sincere interest in those with whom you want to communicate.

Do you know how you sound to others? If you have never recorded your voice and listened to it, buy a tape recorder or rent one. You can rent one in most communities for from three to ten dollars an hour.

How do you sound to others?

Record your voice as if you were talking to a member of your family. Then record it as if you were talking to someone with whom you work. Try to remember a conversation you had during the day and talk into the microphone just as you talked with the other person. Play it back. Ask yourself, "What impression would this voice make on me if I were the other person?"

A business executive who was proud of his open door policy made a recording of his voice as he greeted the people who came to his office during the day. He had thought he was one of the friendliest men in the organization. His door was open to anyone. He was ready to stop anything he was doing and discuss the problems of his employees. When he played back the recording, however, he was shocked. He said, "Why, I sound tense and gruff. No wonder some of my people are ill at ease when they come to my office for advice. I can see now why some of them never came back the second time."

You may use the right words to express your interest in the other person. For instance you might say, "I want to be of service to you." If you say this with enthusiasm, warmth, and sincerity, your listener may be convinced that you are genuinely interested in him. However, if you say the same words in a flat, dull, monotonous voice or, if you sound tense, tired, or grouchy, your voice might very well tell the other person that you don't mean what you say.

See that the tone of your voice demonstrates a real interest in the person with whom you want to communicate and he will be much more interested in hearing what you have to say.

How your actions indicate your interest

Our actions communicate a great deal to other people. For instance, if a husband holds a chair for his wife, stands up when she comes into a room, his action demonstrates an interest in her. On the other hand, if he is slouched down in a chair and doesn't even look up from his newspaper when she talks to him his actions say to her, "I really am not very much interested in you."

During an address before a men's club I discussed the mistakes many of us make when we take the members of our families for granted. Sometimes we aren't as thoughtful as we should be. Perhaps we don't show our appreciation often enough. We can become so involved in our own interests that we forget to demonstrate our interest in those who are close to us.

I asked the men in the audience to raise their hands if they had taken home a little surprise gift to their wives in the past year on any day that was not a birthday, anniversary, or holiday. There wasn't one hand raised in that audience.

I suggested that they stop at a florist on their way home and buy a bouquet for their wives. This would be a welcome surprise, especially if they said, "I brought this to show you I really do appreciate you."

After the dinner meeting several of the men came up to tell me that they liked the suggestions but were afraid to follow it. One said, "My wife would think I'd been up to something for sure." Another said, "My wife would smell my breath." Another said, "My wife would say, 'This isn't my birthday, stupid.'" However, no one questioned the suggestion that we show our appreciation more often than we do.

To achieve the greatest possible success on the human side of communication, it is essential that we show those with whom we want to communicate that we are interested in them. One of the surest ways to do this is through our actions. Therefore, let us demonstrate our thoughtfulness, our courtesy, our kindness, and our appreciation frequently.

How your appearance reflects your interest

Your appearance tells a lot to the other person about your interest in him. If a husband who wouldn't think of going to the office in the morning until he shaves, puts on a clean shirt, a ten-dollar tie and a carefully pressed suit, doesn't even bother to shave when he is home with his wife over the week-end, what does he communicate to her? That she doesn't interest him as much as the people in the office? If he never appeared unshaven before they were married, what does that thick black stubble on his face tell her? She probably is sure he doesn't care as much for her as he once did.

A wife who has been married happily for more than ten years always manages to be dressed attractively when she comes to the door to greet her husband each evening when he comes home from work. Early in their married life he would say in surprise, when he saw her at the door looking so lovely, "Are we having company tonight? Are you expecting someone important?"

She would reply, "Yes, you're the company I'm expecting." Her appearance each evening told him she considered him important to her. This couple have had few communication problems.

When we demonstrate our interest in others, invariably they're interested in anything we have to say.

Summarizing our discussion of the third factor in the ABC's of the human side of communication, we see that we can demonstrate our interest in the person with whom we wish to communicate, (1) through the recognition we give him, (2) through our undivided attention when he is speaking, (3) through the tone of our voice which tells him that we are interested in him, (4) through our actions, and (5) through our appearance.

We must remember that it is not enough to "express" ourselves. It is important, of course, to use words that express our ideas simply, clearly, and understandably. However, we will not "impress" our ideas on the minds of other unless we make other people *want* to listen to us, understand us, and react to what we say the way we want them to. When we achieve this, we communicate successfully.

It is much easier to make people *want* to listen to us, understand us, and react favorably to what we say when we use the ABC technique we have been discussing in this chapter—(A) Study the other person, learn to sense his needs and his reactions. (B) Communicate with him in terms of his own interests, and (C) Show your interest in him.

In the next chapters we will discuss ways this ABC technique can help us communicate more successfully at home and at work.

PART II

SUCCESSFUL COMMUNICATION
IN YOUR HOME

"We are for cooperation, like feet, like hands, like eyelids, like the rows of the upper and lower teeth. To act against one another then is contrary to nature, and it is acting against one another to be vexed and turn away."

MARCUS AURELIUS

Chapter 4

HOW TO WIN YOUR MOST IMPORTANT
"POPULARITY CONTEST"

Most marriages are completely premeditated. Long before the wedding bells start to ring you're thinking, "This is
the doll of my dreams. She's so much fun to be with, to talk to.
She's so interested in everything I do. Life with her will be
great!"

Or you may be thinking, "This is my guy. He's so neat.
Always looks good. He's so considerate. And he's so interested
in me. Life with him is going to be fun!"

In your day dreams you sit side by side, hand in hand, on a
rainbow swinging your feet confidently over the whole wide
world. It's yours, isn't it? At last!

But one morning long after the echo of those wedding bells
has faded away, you awaken and you lie in bed thinking. So
this is married life! After many months it's not at all what you
thought it would be. There he is in those damn wrinkled pa-
jamas, yawning loudly. His clothes are in a pile on the floor
where he dropped them. He's sort of disgusting in some ways.
And he never has much to say any more. He's becoming a
grouch. Why did you ever get into this? It isn't at all like you
thought it would be.

Now he's looking over at you. What's he thinking? Probably wondering why you don't get up and start preparing his breakfast. Actually he's thinking, "Boy, they sure look different in the morning than they do when you call at their mother's house to take them out on a date! I wonder what mood she's in this morning?"

What happens to "togetherness"?

And perhaps he's wondering, too, what happened to the big idea of togetherness that seemed so attractive to him. Togetherness, my eye! You have to have your own way. You've got to be right about everything. He doesn't dare to question anything you do. You're dynamite if he isn't careful about what he says to you. Wow!

You both would like to punch the guy in the nose who dreamed up the line, "And so they were married and lived happily forever after." It doesn't seem to work out that way.

Who's perfect?

But it can and does in many cases, sometimes after a rough period of adjustment. Probably every married man and girl decide at some point that the other partner is not exactly perfect. Very likely each is more or less an I-Lander interested primarily in himself. Perhaps each has habits the other doesn't like, moods the other finds annoying. Each certainly is different from the other, has different interests, thinks and reacts differently. The differences can lead to disagreements, to arguments, to a breakdown in communications, sometimes to such an extent that each speaks to the other only when necessary.

Or each can study the other, learn to sense his needs and his reactions. When this is done, it is easy to communicate with the other person in terms of his own interests.

The wedding bells don't guarantee understanding

Marriage doesn't give us a guarantee that our partner will

listen to us and try to understand us. We have to earn this happy experience through intelligent use of the ABC technique of the human side of communication.

One of the surest ways for a husband and wife to be happier together is to learn to communicate successfully with each other. If they don't, they may have years of misunderstanding, quarrels, and misery.

When they do, they make the necessary adjustments in their approach to each other and they find all the companionship, the fun, the sympathy, the satisfaction and adventure they hoped for.

They found real companionship after several rough years

Bill and Betty Shaw had several years of misunderstandings before they discovered the one small factor which was causing most of their disharmony, their squabbles, and hurt feelings. When they made the necessary adjustments, they found most of the fun of their old companionship came back.

Now they love to talk with each other. They talk out problems. They have fun making plans and doing things together. All because Bill learned about a need Betty had and did something about it.

Usually at seven o'clock each morning the alarm rings in Bill and Betty's bedroom. Bill reaches for the clock on the table between the twin beds and shuts off the alarm. He stretches for a minute or two, then gets up, puts on his robe and goes down to the kitchen to make a pot of coffee. In the meantime, Betty has pulled the covers over her head to shut out the first rays of light. Soon Bill is back with a cup of steaming coffee. He taps the edge of the cup with the spoon and says, "Good morning, you beautiful doll. May I serve your coffee?"

She hates to get up

Reluctantly, Betty peeks out from under the covers. She

says, "Put it on the table, please, Bill. I'll be up in a few minutes."

Bill knows the "few minutes" probably will be ten or fifteen minutes, but he tells her, "Take your time. Enjoy your coffee." And he goes down to the living room and watches a morning news telecast until Betty comes down.

When he was describing this routine to a group of us sitting around the fireplace in his home the other evening he said, "Bringing Betty a cup of coffee each morning has saved our marriage."

This was a very important cup of coffee

One of the women in the group asked, "How could a cup of coffee do that, Bill?"

He said, "As Bob Moore has been pointing out, many a marriage cracks up because a man and his wife don't know how to communicate with each other. This is true. For the first three years of our married life Betty and I had a pretty rough time. We were getting on each other's nerves. We were finding fault with each other constantly and we were quarreling too often.

"One evening sitting right in this room, I said to Betty, 'Our marriage hasn't been a very happy one for you or for me. Living together should be a beautiful experience. But it isn't. Do you think we ought to admit that we made a mistake and call it off?'

She didn't want a divorce

"Betty said, 'I don't want to get a divorce but maybe it would be best for us both. We are two entirely different people.'

"I said, 'We are different. But that shouldn't keep us from enjoying life together. Just what do you think is wrong? We seem to start every day with a quarrel.'

"'That's just it,' Betty said. 'We do start every day growling at each other. But this is my fault. I've thought about it and I believe I know what's wrong.'

"She said, 'This is one of our principal differences. You wake up every morning feeling good. You jump out of bed full of pep. You hum a happy song. And, believe it or not, I resent this.

" 'I hate to get up in the morning. I feel grouchy until I've had my cup of coffee. I'm just one of those people who wakes up slowly.'

She resented her husband every morning for three years

" 'Furthermore, I can't help it but I usually feel gloomy in the morning. If you wonder why I pull the cover over my head, I do it so I won't hear you singing one of your damn cheerful songs. This drives me crazy. I feel like throwing the alarm clock at you. So when I do get up I come out ready for a scrap, as you know.'

"I told Betty it was stupid of me not to realize the way she felt about getting up in the morning. I said there is no reason why she should get up at all. I could make my own breakfast and go off to work while she slept. But this she wouldn't go for.

"So I suggested that I brew the coffee each morning and bring a cup up to her. She could awaken leisurely and have her first sip of coffee in bed. This sounds like a very little thing, but it has been a big one in our lives."

How learning Betty's needs helped Bill save his marriage

Betty agreed with Bill. She said, "If Bill told you the whole story, he would say that I was really bitchy in the morning. The poor fellow couldn't even say, 'Good morning, dear,' and get a cheerful answer. I might say, 'So what's good about it?' or, 'Go away and leave me alone.' Now, however, after that morning cup of coffee in bed, I usually come down with a smile. So even though I'm a real I-Lander, I appreciate Bill's patience and thoughtfulness. We have no trouble communicating successfully. We start off the day in a friendly understanding way and this atmosphere usually continues all day long."

One of the men in the group said, "Bill, you're spoiling my racket. My wife brings me a cup of coffee every morning before I get out of bed!"

Bill replied, "Perhaps you need it just as Betty does. I read recently that several million people usually wake up feeling tired, irritable, and depressed. There's nothing seriously wrong with this—they just happen to be victims of a glandular deficiency which I believe is called partial hypothyroidism. The thyroid glands produce a bit less thyroid hormone than is needed. This slows down physical and mental functions so you don't feel cheerful and bouncy when you wake up.

"If that cup of coffee in bed makes you a happier person and sends you down to the breakfast table in better humor, bringing it to you is one of the smartest things your wife can do! As Bob Moore has been telling us, the first of the three techniques for better communications in the home is to study the other person so you can sense his needs and reactions. If your wife does this with you, she's a smart girl!"

Bill is right. The wife or husband who studies his partner and learns to sense his needs and reactions will be able to push aside the barriers to successful communications.

No two people can be alike in every respect. However, a husband and wife may have entirely different habits and different temperaments, and still enjoy each other's companionship. In a happy marriage, each partner respects the differences of the other and adjusts his thinking and actions in any way that might be necessary. Of course, the wedding ring is not a crystal ball that enables us to read each other's mind and understand each other perfectly. This we have to work at if we are to communicate with each other successfully.

Usually each one wants his marriage to be what he expected it to be

While discussing communications in the home with a minister recently, he said, "The trouble with many husbands and wives who have a rough time getting along together is that they are the I-Landers you talk about. Each wants the marriage to turn out the way *he* expected it to be. Each usually is more concerned with *his* rights than with the other person's happiness. Such couples soon reach the point where nothing seems like fun any more. Then they come to me and complain that they're not in love as they thought they were."

I asked, "What do you tell them?"

He said, "I tell them that most marriages have some rough going. Love is not a natural phenomenon. Passion is. Selfishness is. But love is something that must be cultivated.

Love is "the ultimate concern for another person"

"I find that some of the people who've come to me for help do not have a clear idea of what love is. I explain that love is the ultimate concern for another person.

"This is not easy for an I-Lander to achieve. Usually he is too self-centered. When he does cultivate an ultimate concern for another person, he becomes a We-Lander and living with another person becomes fun again."

He said, "Most ministers, priests, and rabbis do what we do —we counsel with the prospective bride and groom before we marry them. For instance, I review the marriage service. I tell the man and woman about to be married that God, through his Apostles, has instructed those who enter into this relationship to cherish a mutual esteem and love; to bear with each other's infirmities and weaknesses; to comfort each other in sickness, in trouble, and sorrow; in honesty and in industry to provide for each other and for their household in temporal things; to pray for and encourage each other in the things which pertain to God; and to live together as the heirs of the Grace of Life.

"I emphasize the fact that they are to cherish 'a mutual esteem and love for each other' and they are to 'bear with each other's weaknesses and infirmities.'

"We all try to prepare them for the rough going. But this does not always work. My own sister and her husband came to me a few years ago and told me that they were thinking of getting a divorce.

"During my conference with them I found that their trouble was a breakdown in communications. During our discussion they would interrupt each other, criticize each other. Each claimed the other insisted on having his own way. I suggested that they think it over for a few weeks and that during this period they ask each other this question whenever either wanted to do something the other didn't want to do— Is this really important to you?

A key question helps two good people communicate more successfully

"You'd be surprised how this question helps people understand each other. As you know, many argue about things that are not at all important. Each insists on having his own way. One angry word leads to another and soon they can be miles apart in bitterness. However, this key question can bring them together.

"For instance, if the wife wants to go to the movies and the husband wants to stay home and watch the wrestling matches on television, the wife might ask, 'Is this really important to you?'

"The husband might reply, 'No, I don't really care about the wrestling matches, but I don't want to go to the movies tonight. Is going to the movies really important to you?'

"The wife might say, 'No, going to the movies isn't important to me, but I don't want to watch those darn wrestling matches.'

What happens then? Instead of being angry with each other, they decide to do something else and do it together."

My minister friend said, "You emphasize the necessity of studying the other person in order to learn to sense his needs and his reactions. The key question I just suggested can help one person study another, especially during the critical moments when there is a difference of opinion.

"My sister and her husband tell me this question has helped them. She said now whenever they have a difference of opinion they sit down and talk it over. One will ask the other, 'Is this really important to you?' The answers to this question helps each understand the other's point of view and this, of course, promotes more successful communication"

Your marriage partner will listen to you— when you interest him

It is evident that the marriage ceremony does not guarantee that the other person will listen to us, understand us and react as we want him to. We must remember that the other's mind is his own private domain. He lets us in only when we interest him.

While discussing the reasons for breakdowns in communications in the home with a Catholic priest, he said, "Even though marriage is a Holy Sacrament, unfortunately it does not bring happiness to everyone. It seems there is bound to be some friction when two people who are more or less strangers to each other realize that they are going to live together for the rest of their lives.

When you insist on "your rights" you may lose your happiness

"If they are self-centered, and so many evidently are, they begin to insist on their rights. They begin to magnify the other's deficiencies. Soon hate comes in and then they're lost."

He said, "When I was studying for the priesthood we were

taught not to stand on our rights. In a rectory, for instance, a curate, even when he thinks he's right, should give in to a priest. Or a priest could give in to the curate instead of standing on his rights. They should do this for a higher ideal—to preserve peace in the rectory. A man and his wife should do this in the home as well.

Look for, and accentuate, the good in each other

"We try to tell them this in the conferences we have with them before the marriage ceremony. And in our Cana Conferences we show the couple that they must respect each other, try to understand each other, look for and accentuate the good in each other."

How can one show respect and understanding of another person? How can one accentuate the good in another? Through the human side of successful communication.

If every married couple would use the ABC technique, they would communicate successfully and "live happily ever after."

If you are married, you can win your most important popularity contest—the contest for popularity with your husband or wife—by using the ABC technique every day—(A) Study the other person, learn to sense his needs and his reactions. (B) Communicate with him in terms of his own interests, and (C) show your interest in him.

In the next chapters we will discuss specific application of these techniques. We will see how they can make married life a truly satisfying experience.

"Words will not say what I yearn to say—
They will not walk as I want them to,
But they stumble and fall in the path of the way
Of my telling my love for you."

JAMES WHITCOMB RILEY

Chapter 5

FOR MEN ONLY—
HOW TO COMMUNICATE MORE SUCCESSFULLY
WITH YOUR WIFE THAN THE OTHER MEN
IN HER LIFE

When Jerry Walsh was driving his wife Grace home from a party, he said, "You sure were a ball of fire with the other boys this evening. How come you seem so bored with me now?"

Grace said, "I'm not bored, just tired. Besides, the other men who were there this evening happened to be interesting. And by the way, they seemed eager to listen to what I had to say. You seldom are these days."

Jerry said, "I've got a lot on my mind. And besides, when do you ever listen to me? You're always running the damn vacuum cleaner or rattling the dishes when I want to say something to you."

"Say something interesting," she suggests

"That isn't exactly true," Grace said. "However, let's not argue. Say something interesting to me and I'll listen."

Jerry asked, "What could I say that would interest you?"

Grace suggested, "Suppose you tell me what you thought of

the party tonight. And then ask me to tell you what I think of everyone who was there, especially the other women. Then you sit back and listen to me!"

When Jerry was telling me about this incident, he said, "I don't know what is happening to us. Before we were married we seemed to have so much to talk about. Now we're a couple of clams. Grace says I never tell her anything any more. I say she wouldn't listen if I did. She doesn't seem interested in my affairs. She just wants to yak, yak about what she did all day. I guess we're probably like a lot of other married people settling down to a dull existence."

Why do communications between husband and wife sometimes bog down after several years of married life?

Grace and Jerry had a lot to talk about before they were married and they listened to each other because they *wanted* to. Why did they *want* to? Because everything either one of them had to say was interesting to the other. What has happened in the several years since they walked down the aisle together?

Who is to blame when there is a breakdown in communications between husbands and wives? One wife said, "Nearly every woman I know complains that her husband never tells her anything. Mine doesn't either." This wife said she believes women are at fault. She thinks the principal reason husbands don't have much to say to their wives is that women are poor listeners. I don't agree with this. I'm sure women will listen to anything to which they *want* to listen. In my opinion, we husbands may be to blame when communications break down in the home. Often we don't make our wives *want* to listen to us.

Usually we are I-Landers. We think of our own needs and our own interests and are inclined to assume that our wives are interested in us. They are to some extent. But they're probably I-Landers, too. They have needs they expect us to satisfy.

Their interest in us may be in proportion to the way we satisfy their needs.

Your wife needs companionship

What are these needs? A recent survey showed that most wives married for companionship. This is their primary need. They may work at home alone all day. Or they may go to business. But whom do they see who is interested in them? They need a husband they can talk to in their leisure hours, someone who shares their interests, someone who listens to them and understands them.

She wants to be told she is right occasionally

Also they need a husband who respects their opinions. They want to be right about some things, at least occasionally. They resent the feeling of inferiority they are given by a husband who corrects them continually. Yet many husbands are inclined to do just this—to point out to our ever loving wives where they are wrong.

One wife said, "I think my husband is afraid to admit he's wrong about anything and I'm right because he doesn't want me to get the idea I'm smarter than he is."

She wants to be appreciated

Finally, every wife wants to know that her husband appreciates her, even when she doesn't stay on her diet, even though the beauty shop doesn't come up with exactly the right shade of red in her hair tinting job.

A wife's needs aren't many, but how often does a husband study his wife and learn to sense her needs and her reactions? A husband is more likely to be thinking of his own needs.

He comes home after a busy day and his wife calls, "Hello dear, I'm glad to see you're home. Let me tell you what happened at Harriet's today."

While the wife is talking, her husband is going over to the

clothes closet and he is putting away his hat and coat and taking out his paper.

And, while she's still talking, he walks into the living room, sits down and opens the paper to the Wall Street prices or to the sports page and he reads it while she is talking to him.

He isn't listening

Then she asks him two or three times, "Will you go?" and he doesn't listen. Finally she comes over and perhaps she takes the paper away from him. Then she asks, "Will you go, dear?" He looks up and with a hurt expression, says, "Will I go where?"

She mutters, "You're impossible!" She walks away and goes into the kitchen to start preparing dinner.

When he finishes his paper, he calls out to her, "By the way, let me tell you what happened to me at the office today! We had a meeting and I suggested some brilliant ideas."

She doesn't listen to him

The faucet turns on. The dishes are rattling. He protests, "You're not listening to me!" She says, "Oh yes I am. I can hear you." But she isn't listening. Why? Because he didn't listen to her.

Now the first technique that I suggest for effective communication in the home is the technique of really listening. When you come home, if your wife starts to say, "Dear, let me tell you what Harriet said today during our bridge game," listen to her immediately. Instead of taking off your hat and coat and walking to the coat closet to hang them, just stop where you are, with your coat half off and hat in your hand and say, "Tell me!"

She'll talk for a few minutes and then she'll notice that you're standing in the hall with your coat half off and your hat in your hand and she'll say, "Oh, excuse me darling, hang up your hat and coat. Come on in and I'll tell you the rest of it." Then you hang up your things and go into the living room.

Don't sneak a peek at the newspaper as you go in! Just sit there and listen to her.

Now she wants to listen to you

The first thing you know she will have finished telling you about her experience with Harriet and then she'll say, "Now tell me about your day!" And she will listen to you because she *wants* to!

Getting someone to listen to you isn't easy. Remember that Professor Ralph Nichols pointed out that we speak at the rate of 100 to 125 words a minute. But the mental cruising speed of the person listening to us is 400 to 500 words a minute. So you see, while you're talking to your wife, she could be thinking rings around you. And this she will do unless you make her *want* to listen to you.

If you want your wife to listen to you, listen attentively to her whenever she talks to you. Stop whatever you're doing. Look directly at her. Show her she has your complete attention. Encourage her to discuss her problems with you. Ask questions to be sure you understand her. Show her you're interested in her work, in her friends, in her ideas, in anything she wants to tell you. Then watch how enthusiastic she is about you and how she listens willingly whenever you speak to her!

By listening to your wife you learn what interests her and how to talk to her in terms of her interests.

We husbands are inclined to show our superiority

One of the causes of the cold war situation in many homes is something that probably comes from a masculine inferiority complex. Many of us husbands evidently think we have to show "the little woman" how smart we are, how superior to members of the so-called weaker sex. So we never hesitate to tell our wives they're wrong about something. This enables us to reassert our superiority—this drives our wives crazy.

It may start this way. A wife tells her husband she is going to rearrange the furniture in the living room. She thinks the sofa would look better on the other side of the room. Her husband says, "You're wrong! It looks better where it is."

When she tells some friends, "We paid $300 for that new television set," he might say, "No we didn't. We paid $295 for it." Don't do this. Let her be right for five dollars!

Whenever you have a difference of opinion, try to see her side of it. And never tell her flatly that she's wrong. Seldom is one person completely wrong and the other completely right.

If you don't let her be right, she will be trying to prove that you are wrong and her mind won't be open to you at all.

Don't tell her she's wrong!

Even if she goes to such an extreme that some morning at breakfast she says to you, "You're the homeliest husband a woman ever had!" don't tell her she's wrong. It would be a natural inclination for you to say, "Well, you're not so hot yourself." But this, of course, may not be true.

Instead of that, help her to be right. When she says, "You're the homeliest husband a woman ever had," you say, "You're probably right. You didn't get much of a bargain when you married me, did you? I'm certainly no Gregory Peck or Cary Grant."

She'll love you!

When you say that, what will happen? What will she say? She'll look at you and an expression of fondness will come into her eyes. She'll say, "I didn't really mean what I said. You know, we girls have certain days when we're irritable and feel a little mean. I had to take it out on someone and you were here, so I took it out on you. Please forgive me. Believe me, I wouldn't trade you for a thousand Gregory Pecks! Cary Grant? No, not even for him!"

So help her to be right. When you do, you demonstrate your interest in her and she will be predisposed to listen favorably to anything you have to say.

Make it fun

Helping your wife be right need not be a big burden to you. Why not make it fun? Sam West does. When Sam and his wife Lillian were in Hawaii some time ago, they saw two taxicabs collide at a street corner. No one was hurt, the paint was hardly scratched. But the Hawaiian cab drivers got out and started arguing.

As Sam explained it, the cab drivers used only two words during the ten or fifteen minutes he and Lillian watched them wave their arms and shout at each other.

One of the words was a contraction of "What's the matter?" This became "Whatsamatta?"

Here is the way the argument went: The first driver shouted, "Whasamatta you?"

The second shouted back, "Whasamatta me? Whasamatta you!"

The first one retorted, "Whasamatta me? Whasamatta you!"

This went on and on. First one would shout, "Whasamatta me? Whasamatta you!" And the other would shout back the same question and the same accusation that the other was the one in the wrong.

Learn to laugh at yourself

As Sam and Lillian walked away, Sam said, "You know, Lillian, you and I have engaged in similar word battles. Our words were different, but the music was the same. Each one of us tried to prove the other wrong. I'm most to blame. In the future I'm going to try to remember the 'Whasamatta you' boys. Maybe I can learn to laugh at myself before I take something unimportant too seriously."

Sam tells me that now when he and Lillian have a disagreement or when he's inclined to criticize Lillian for something she's said or done, he remembers those taxi drivers in Hawaii. Instead of saying, "You're wrong." Or, "How could you do such a stupid thing!" he smiles and says, "Whasamatta you?"

Lillian will reply, "Whasamatta me? Whasamatta you!" and they both have a good laugh.

They now laugh at many situations which formerly might have brewed an argument, especially if he thoughtlessly tried to show his long-suffering partner how wrong a wife can be.

Respect your wife's opinions

Help your wife be right. Never say, "You're wrong!" If you don't agree with her, say, "I respect your point of view. You're probably right." Then ask, "Would you like to know my opinion?" When she tells you she would, you know she'll listen to you and try to understand you.

If you ignore her opinion, tell her how wrong she is, and insist on explaining "the facts" of the situation, her mind very likely will be cruising at the rate of 400 to 500 words a minute far away from you and whatever you have to say.

Show that you appreciate her

The third technique for communicating successfully with your wife is one of the most important. It is a simple technique. But we are so busy with our own interests we sometimes neglect this. This technique is—show your wife that you appreciate her.

Instead of thinking, as you drive home from work, of all the things that are wrong with the little woman waiting there for you, think of all the things you like about her. Instead of thinking: She's hard to get along with. She isn't as much fun as she used to be. You don't like the new hairdo, or the red hair she's wearing these days, think of her gentleness and warmth and kindness and the many other good qualities she has.

Take home a present tonight

Stop in a gift shop on the way home and pick up some small gift for her. It doesn't have to be expensive. When you walk in tonight, tell her you brought the little gift because you've been thinking that she's pretty wonderful and you appreciate her.

Phone her during the day occasionally and ask her to go out to dinner with you. Tell her you were thinking about her and felt it would be good for her to get away from the house and relax with you. This will communicate to her the fact that you do not take her for granted, that you appreciate all her thought and effort in keeping an attractive home for you.

If you do this, do you think you will have any difficulty getting her to listen to you or to understand what you're saying? You will experience the pleasure of communicating successfully with a wife who is interested in every word you say.

There are so many things to appreciate

Is it necessary to bring home evidence of your appreciation every day? Of course it isn't. But let your wife know each day that you appreciate something about her or something she has done. The dinner that you enjoyed. The way she rearranged the living room. The curtains she made. The sound of her voice. The sparkle in her eyes. Tell her often that you do appreciate her and you'll seldom have any trouble communicating with your appreciated partner.

Some wives are starved for expressions of appreciation

Some wives are so starved for appreciation they tell their husbands, "You don't love me." If your wife says this, she may be thinking, "No matter how hard I try to make you comfortable and happy, you take everything for granted. I wonder whether you appreciate anything I do!"

Surprise her with little tokens of appreciation

One husband surprises his wife with two red roses from time to time, just as he did when they were engaged. He has a lot more money now and could buy roses by the dozen, but the two roses have a special meaning.

Another husband brings his wife the perfume she likes, but won't buy for herself because she thinks it's too expensive.

One husband brought his wife a box of candy every pay day. This proved to be a mistake. Don't get into a gift giving routine. One pay day he was in a hurry to get home and didn't stop for the usual token of his appreciation. When he walked into the house, she asked, "Where's my candy?" What started out to be a thoughtful gesture of appreciation had become just a routine supply of candy. Plan to surprise her at different times with something that will show her you're glad she decided to walk down that aisle with you.

A sincere word of appreciation each day will keep the divorce court far away.

How to get along with your wife—and live longer

For more successful communication with your wife, try the three techniques we've just discussed:

1. Listen attentively whenever she talks to you. This provides the companionship she needs and enables you to learn her interests and communicate with her in terms of her interests.
2. Help her to be right.
3. Show her you appreciate her. When you help her to be right and express your appreciation, you leave no doubt in her mind that you are interested in her.

Make this 30-day test

If you are not now using these techniques for more effective communication in your home, try them for the next thirty days. If, after thirty days, when you come home your wife meets you at the door and says, "Come on in, dear, you must have had a busy day." If she says, "Let me take your hat and coat." If she takes your hat and coat and hangs them up and says, "Go into the living room and sit in your favorite chair before the fireplace." If you walk into the room and see a cheerful fire crackling in the fireplace and you sit in your favorite chair and she comes over and lifts your feet and puts them on the hassock. If she unties your shoes and puts on your slippers and then says, "Just a minute, dear. I'll fix your favorite cocktail." If she goes into the kitchen and brings out your favorite cocktail, pours it for you, and hands you your pipe filled with your favorite tobacco . . .

Now if this happens, drop me a note and say, "These human side of successful communication techniques really work."

"*I would give up all my genius, and all my books, if there were only some woman somewhere who cared whether or not I came home late for dinner.*"

IVAN S. TURGENEV

Chapter 6

FOR WOMEN ONLY—
HOW TO COMMUNICATE SO SUCCESSFULLY
WITH YOUR HUSBAND THAT YOU WRAP HIM
AROUND YOUR DAINTY LITTLE FINGER

Women are more intelligent than men. They have more imagination. They are far more intuitive. Every husband knows this. That's why he would like to have his wife become the real boss of the family, providing she bosses him with an understanding, respectful, and loving touch.

When she does, she gets all the companionship, fun, and adventure she hoped for.

When she becomes heavy-handed, however, and starts to throw brickbats instead of verbal bouquets, she usually gets back exactly what she throws. Her chance to take the high place in her husband's life that she might have had goes out the window and she just becomes what the cartoonists picture as an unpleasant "ball and chain."

You might ask, "Can a really intelligent woman say and do things that would be so unpleasant to her husband that they would make him dislike her, perhaps even hate her?

"And could the same woman simply by changing her communication technique, have a happy, satisfying marriage?"

One wife has only peaceful coexistence,
the other has a happy home

The answer to both questions is "Yes." Consider these two examples of communication between husband and wife. In one case the couple quarrels frequently, their marriage has become a struggle for peaceful coexistence. In the other, the marriage has been a happy one for more than twelve years.

Two husbands came home about an hour late one evening. In one instance the wife did not come to the door. She was sitting in the living room when her husband came in. She was smoking a cigarette and reading a magazine. She looked up and said, "No telephones in your office? If you had been here when you said you would be, you might have had a good steak. Now it will be as tough as shoe leather, but it's your fault, you know. Don't blame me!"

In the other case the wife met her husband at the door. She kissed him warmly. She said, "I was so worried about you, dear. I love you so much. If anything happened to you, I don't know what I'd do."

She continued, "Let me take your hat and coat. You must be very tired. Why don't you relax in the living room and I'll make you a drink."

Which of these women do you think has an unhappy married life?

You're right—the first one.

If you were a man, would you be interested in listening to anything the first one had to say to you? You probably would have to force yourself to listen because you would be so hurt by her completely I-Lander greeting.

If you were a man and you were greeted by your wife the way the second girl greeted her husband, you probably would relax completely with an open mind and a sympathetic heart, ready to listen to anything she had to say.

Thoughtless communication mistakes can wreck a marriage

There are several communication mistakes which a wife can make thoughtlessly and virtually wreck her marriage. And there are several techniques which can just about guarantee the success of the marriage. The mistakes are illustrated by this next case history which a prominent midwestern psychologist discussed with me. We will call him "Dr. Church," which is not his name, so as not to embarrass his client. We will call his client "Mrs. Emma Green."

Mrs. Green had heard Dr. Church lecture at a woman's club on the art of making marriage successful. She phoned for a consultation. When she came into the office, she said, "I think I'm going to have a nervous breakdown. My husband has told me to get out of the house. He even said I should go as far away from him as possible. He said he'd be glad if I went all the way to California! I'm so upset I don't know what to do."

Dr. Church asked, "When did he say all this? Please describe the circumstances as nearly as you can remember them and tell me exactly what he did say."

She said, "It was last night. He came home with a long face as usual, hung up his hat and coat, took his paper and went into the living room and sat down. He opened the paper and started to read it. I went out to the kitchen to prepare his dinner. He didn't say a word to me."

Dr. Church asked, "What did you say to him?"

A wife angry because she had none of the companionship she wanted

She said, "I came out of the kitchen and said, 'So this is the togetherness they talk about! You come in and plunk yourself down in a chair and start to read your darn newspaper and don't even say a word. You act as though I'm not even here. Well, you listen to me. I work just as hard as you do and I'm

just as important around here as you are and if you don't
think so, I can leave right now.'

"He said, 'Well go ahead and leave.' He didn't even look up
from his paper.

"I asked, 'What's so important in the paper that you can't
put it down?'

"He said, 'I'm reading the financial page.'

"I laughed. I said, 'Reading the financial page—after all the
money you've lost in the stock market. You ought to forget that
stuff and maybe you'd be in better humor.'

"He didn't say a word. He just kept reading. I went back into
the kitchen and continued preparing dinner. Then I said, 'Your
dinner is ready. Come and eat it if you want it.'

He read the paper at the dinner table

"He came to the table and he brought his newspaper with
him. He sat there reading the paper and eating. He's done this
before and it always makes me mad. Last night I said, 'Now
look, if you're going to read that newspaper while you're sitting at the dinner table, I'm going to leave you.'

"He didn't put down his paper. He just said, 'Well, go ahead!'

"This made me burn. I said, 'I will. And I'll go far away!'

"He said, 'Good. The farther the better!'

"I said, 'All right, if you feel that way, I'll go all the way to
California.'

"He said, 'Good. I'll buy the ticket!'

"I said, 'If you're that anxious to get rid of me, I'll go tonight.'

"He said, 'It's OK with me. I'll help you pack.'

"You see, doctor, he doesn't want me. He wants me to leave
my home and go as far away as possible. I don't know what to
do. I thought you might be able to help me."

Dr. Church asked, "Did he buy the ticket to California?" Mrs.
Green answered, "No, he didn't."

Then the doctor asked, "Did he help you pack?" Mrs. Green
said, "No, he didn't."

What was her husband really communicating?

Dr. Church asked, "Did it ever occur to you, Mrs. Green, that your husband did not mean the words he used? He didn't help you pack. He didn't buy the ticket to California. Perhaps he was very tired after a rough day at work and wanted a short period of relaxation. He evidently needed some things that you did not give him. Your whole conversation with him was one-sided—all about what you wanted.

"Furthermore," Dr. Church added, "you made several mistakes that can jeopardize a wife's relationship with her husband. You made him feel unimportant by emphasizing just how important you thought you were. You showed a lack of respect for him when you criticized his unfortunate experience in the stock market. And you insisted on your rights to companionship and attention instead of doing the things that would make him want to give you companionship and attention."

Mrs. Green asked, "What should I do?"

Dr. Church said, "Let's start by trying to change your attitude toward your husband. Instead of thinking about what you want from him, let's think about what you can do for him to make him a bit happier. Take a simple thing—the food you prepare for his dinner. How do you usually decide what to prepare?"

Mrs. Green said, "I try to give him a well-balanced meal. I fix what is good for him."

The doctor asked, "Does he have any favorite dish, something that he likes particularly—perhaps something that you know he enjoyed before you were married?"

Mrs. Green thought for a minute and then she said, "Yes. He's a Southerner and his mother used to make pecan pie for him and he loved it."

The doctor asked, "Have you ever baked a pecan pie?"

She said, "No, I haven't."

He asked, "Can you bake this type of pie?"

She said, "Yes, I'm proud of the fact that I'm a good cook. I certainly could make a good pecan pie."

Dr. Church suggested, "Why don't you bake one for him today. Don't say anything about it to him when he comes home. But put on one of your best dresses. Make yourself look as attractive as you possibly can. Have that pie that he likes so much ready and serve it as your dessert. Call me tomorrow and tell me what happened."

What happened when she followed the psychologist's advice?

The next day Mrs. Green called. She said, "I didn't believe a pecan pie could make so much difference, doctor. When my husband came home last night he went into the living room, sat down and read his paper as usual. But I didn't complain this time. I simply prepared the dinner and told him when it was ready. He brought his paper to the table and read it all during the dinner. When I served him a big piece of pecan pie, he was still reading the paper. He didn't look at the pie.

"However, when he bit into the first forkful of that pie, he put down the newspaper and looked across at me and said, 'Why, this is pecan pie!'

"Then he said, 'You remembered how much I liked this, didn't you?' I told him 'Yes, I did.'

"Then he looked at me and said, 'Why, you're all dressed up. Are you going out tonight?'

"I said, 'No, I just wanted to look especially nice for you. And I apologize for being stupid. From now on when you want to read your paper when you come home, you go ahead and read it. I'll try to be more understanding because I love you.'"

She found it so much easier to get what she wanted when she made her husband want it, too

Then she said, "The most wonderful thing happened. He came around to my side of the table and put his arms around me and kissed me. He hadn't done this for a long, long time. He said, 'I'm the one who's been stupid. And I apologize to you. I have been having a rough time at work but I shouldn't let that interfere with our relationship. From now on we're going to have more fun together just as we used to have!' "

Emma Green said, "Dr. Church, I could hardly believe it. How could a little pecan pie make all that difference?"

Dr. Church said, "It wasn't the pecan pie, Mrs. Green. You just changed your way of communicating with him. You had been trying to get what you wanted through nagging and criticism and insisting on your rights. Last night you made your husband feel that he is important to you.

"Instead of asking, 'What can he do to make me happy?' you asked yourself, 'What can I do to make him happy?' And you did what you could last evening. You keep this up and you won't need my services any more."

The smart wife will remember the mistakes that Emma Green made and avoid them. She will not make her husband feel like an unimportant person. She will not show any disrespect for him or his judgment. She will not insist on getting his attention and his interest because it is her right.

It is so much easier for an intelligent wife to get everything she wants from her husband, to wrap him around her dainty little finger, by using the ABC Human Side of Communication technique.

Three things every husband needs

Study your husband. What does he need that you can give him? Principally he needs three things: He's a man and he loves you so he needs to feel he is an important person to you. He needs to know that you respect him. And he needs evidence of your affection.

When you communicate with your husband in a way that shows him he is important to you, shows him you respect him and are fond of him, you are communicating with him in terms of his own interests. And you are demonstrating your interest in him. You can be sure he will *want* to listen to you and understand you.

Why should any wife choose to argue, nag, and fight with her husband when she can enjoy happy companionship by doing these three things:

1. Show that he is an important person to you.
2. Show that you respect him.
3. Show your affection for him in many ways.

Show him that he is an important person to you

One wife I know always watches for her husband's car to come into the driveway when he comes home from work. She goes to the door to meet him. She wears something attractive and colorful. She may say, "I missed you today." Or she may say, "It's lonesome around here without you." She makes him feel important.

Another wife has established a rule in her house that during the first hour after her husband has come home from work, the children are not to come into the living room. This girl was in business herself before marrying her husband. She knows that he can be very tired after a hectic day. So she has set aside an hour of relaxation which she shares with him. During this period they have a cocktail or two and quietly discuss the events of the day.

When friends say, "But don't your children come first with you?" she says, "No. Why should I cater to them and neglect my husband? They'll be leaving here when they grow up just as I left my mother's home, and where would I be? Sitting here with a husband who is a stranger? Trying to pick up where we left off before the kids were born? Not on your life. This is not for me! I love my children, but in their place—and their place comes after my husband."

Remember that your husband probably is an I-lander. Your opinion of him is very important to him. Don't let thoughtless words or acts belittle him. For instance, don't make the mistake one wife makes who hands her husband a bag of garbage as he leaves for the office in the morning. He leaves the house in his $150 suit carrying a bag of leaky garbage. He says, "In my office, I'm a big shot. At home I'm just the boy who carries out the garbage."

Send your husband out in the morning feeling that he is a very important person to you. Tell him how good he looks. Tell him that you've been thinking about some of the ideas that he discussed the night before and you think they're great. Send him out feeling that he could conquer the whole world—and he'll want to do this for you!

Show him that you respect him

When he talks to you, shut off the vacuum cleaner and listen. And listen with your complete attention. Never let your glance wander away while he is talking.

Don't interrupt him and finish his sentences just because your mind is speeding far ahead of his words. Listen patiently, especially when he is talking about himself and his work.

Show him that you are interested in his work by asking questions about it.

One wife said, "After a bad day at the shop my husband comes home and cries to me about the trouble he has with the foreman he doesn't like. I used to hate to hear all his troubles. But who else does he have to talk things out with? I've learned to sympathize with him and I try to help him see the good side of things. This he appreciates."

If he should lose money on a stock market investment, don't criticize his judgment. Show your understanding by saying, "This can happen to anyone. It's past, so let's not worry about it. Your judgment is very good in most things." Don't criticize his mistakes or accentuate his shortcomings. Accentuate his good points, the many things he does that are successful. Show your respect for him and you will find that he has a deep respect for you.

Show your affection for him in many ways

They say that Mrs. Winston Churchill was five minutes late for her wedding and Winston was so glad to see her that he shook hands with her when she took her place at his side at the altar. He has been glad to see her ever since because she finds many ways to show her affection for him.

For instance, even though they have been married for more than fifty years, she reaches out and takes his hand and holds it as they walk side by side down the street. They have no trouble communicating with each other.

Some cynics say that it is natural for husbands to become bored and lose interest in their wives a few years after the wedding. This does happen in some cases, but it is not "natural." I have known a number of cases where husbands had affairs with other women or patronized call girls. Usually the wife was the Emma Green type who thought she was doing her duty when she kept a good home, cooked well-balanced meals, was a good mother for his children. She felt she had a right to insist on her husband's respect and affection. One of the men said, however, "How can you love someone who has been nagging you, or want to go to bed with someone who has just been criticizing you and calling attention to your shortcomings?"

The wise wife doesn't assume that she will always have her husband's affection, that he will never be interested in other girls. She gets all the love she wants by demonstrating to her husband her own affection for him in many ways.

Surprise him in pleasant little ways

One wife mails little personal notes to her husband at his office from time to time. When he's going through a stack of business mail he finds an envelope marked "personal." He recognizes his wife's handwriting. When he opens it he finds a short note which might simply read, "I miss you and I love you. I'm always lonesome until I hear your car in the driveway."

I've never known this husband to show an interest in any other girl.

Another successful wife buys her husband little presents many times during the year not just on special occasions. She places one of them on his dinner plate or she might have one on the pillow of his bed. Attached to each one is a card which has this message: "To the man I hope to marry some day after living this life of sin with him." After nearly ten years of marriage he still gets a big kick out of this. His wife has no trouble communicating with him.

Have a "tender room"

Psychologists say that many marriages crack up in the bedroom. Some believe the cause of crackups is sexual incompatibility. I don't believe this at all. In my opinion, many marriages do fail in the bedroom but the failure is due to a breakdown in communications in this room.

Too many people quarrel in their bedrooms. Or they discuss the routine problems of the day in the bedroom, perhaps while they're lying in bed they may argue, or find fault with each other, or even nag each other. If any of this happens, how can either feel affectionate towards the other?

An intelligent wife will make her bedroom a "tender room." She will suggest to her husband, "Let's agree that in this one room in our house, we'll never discuss business, family troubles, or talk about anyone else but ourselves. Under no circumstances will we ever argue or criticize each other or bring up anything that would be unpleasant. This one room will be our 'tender room.' Here we will be gentle and considerate towards each other always. This will be a haven of tenderness for us."

As you know, there is much more to love than passion alone. As a minister friend said, "Love is the ultimate consideration for another person. When you make your bedroom a 'tender room' and in this one room in your home always have the ultimate consideration for your husband, you will demonstrate your interest in him in a way that will keep him very much interested in you. You can be sure he will have the ultimate consideration for you!"

If you aren't using these techniques for greater success on the human side of communication in your home, try them.

Try these three techniques for successful communication with your husband

1. Show your husband that he is an important person to you every day of your life.

2. Show him that you respect him.

3. Show him your affections in many, many ways.

When you do, you will find that he is anxious to come home to you. He will listen willingly whenever you speak to him. He will be very much interested in understanding you and he'll be predisposed to consider favorably everything you have to say. In short, you will have successful communications in your home. You will be able to wrap him around your dainty little finger and he'll love it.

*"Children begin by loving their parents;
as they grow older they judge them;
sometimes they forgive them."*

OSCAR WILDE

Chapter 7

FOR PARENTS—
HOW SUCCESSFUL COMMUNICATION CAN
HELP YOU RAISE WONDERFUL CHILDREN

An army engineer who served in Korea and in the Southwestern section of this country told me he was impressed by the fact that American Indian children and Korean children never cry. He said, "You know that the Indian mothers and Korean mothers carry their babies on their backs wherever they go. This gives them a sense of security American children do not have."

He said, "I've seen a line of Koreans pass close to an enemy outpost at night, the mothers carrying the children on their backs. And there was never any question that the babies might cry. They just don't."

Do children sometimes cry because they feel insecure?

"We have two children," my friend said, "and they cry. They cry when they're alone and feel insecure. Crying brings my wife or me or the baby sitter. They're reassured by our interest and stop crying. Later they learn this is a good way to get attention. American children get away with murder when they

111

cry, probably because we parents have a guilty feeling about them."

I asked, "What do you mean by 'a guilty feeling'?"

He said, "In the early part of a baby's life an American mother seldom keeps it close to her, as the Indian and Korean mothers do. Some American mothers work. Many have a wide variety of outside interests so they leave the children with relatives or baby sitters. I think this gives mothers a sub-conscious feeling of guilt. The fathers feel this, too, and both parents compensate for it by being over-protective and over-indulgent as the children grow up.

"Instead of giving a child a sense of security, this makes him feel insecure and inadequate. Children resent this. Some who don't feel secure at home reject their parents' ideas and seek security in a neighborhood gang where the leader exercises the firm control over members that their own parents thought would be too severe for 'little Johnny.' Some of our juvenile delinquents, you know, come from our better homes!"

Children need sense of security

My friend is an engineer not a psychologist. However, every psychologist would agree that he is right in at least one respect —children do need a strong sense of security.

Perhaps American children do have less in their early months than Korean or Indian children. If they are born in a hospital, and most American children are today, they're taken away from their mothers and placed "in storage" in a room full of babies. They're brought to their mothers for feeding and then back they go to a clean, sterile, but impersonal world. When they're taken home, they're lowered into a crib and left alone again.

Sometimes they're left with relatives or strangers while their mothers are away. In their first months some are alone most of the time—in a strange new world.

Perhaps my friend was right when he said they cry because

they feel insecure. And possibly this feeling of insecurity stays in the subconscious mind of some children all their lives.

As they grow up and learn to talk, the parents can strengthen their feeling of security by using the ABC technique for successful communication in our homes.

How to communicate successfully with your children

For instance, the first step in the ABC technique is "study the other person. Learn to sense his needs and his reactions." What are the needs of your children? They need security based on a close relationship with parents who love them well enough to discipline them. They need self-respect based on their performance as responsible members of the family. They need guidance that helps them develop self-direction and self-discipline.

To communicate successfully with your children, start at the cradle to listen to them

Some parents have few communication problems in their homes. The children listen attentively when the parents speak and freely discuss their own plans and their own problems. Usually this happy situation is not accidental. Someone planned to have it this way. When I asked the father of several children the secret of his success in promoting an atmosphere of relaxed and confident communication in his home, he said, "You've got to start from the cradle to listen to your children. If they learn when they're little that they can come to you and tell you what's on their mind, they get used to talking with you. They learn that you will listen and understand them. They try to do this when you talk to them."

Why there is little understanding communication in some homes

This father, who is the training director of a well-known firm, said, "The downfall of communication in homes today is threefold: parents are too lazy to listen to their children, they both work, in some cases because they'd rather have more of the material luxuries of life than have well-adjusted children, and because they will not take the time to discipline their children and teach them how to discipline themselves."

When the American mother of the year was interviewed on a radio program, she was asked, "What is the secret of your success? Do you have any success formula that you can pass on to other mothers?"

She said, "Yes. Love your children with all your heart, but love them enough to discipline them."

The discipline part of this formula is difficult for some parents to follow. It seems to be for Linda's mother (whom we shall call Sylvia to avoid embarrassing her). Sylvia belongs to a number of clubs and is active in community affairs. She often drops Linda off at a baby sitter's home. Here, Linda, who is six, is a perfect lady. At home she has tantrums and cries when she doesn't get her way immediately. Her mother waits on her, gives her everything she wants. What makes the difference in this child?

Children appreciate an intelligent listener

Her baby sitter is a mature, intelligent French girl who has been in this country many years. She said she remembers the long conversations she had with her mother in her early years. This she loved. She wonders why American mothers are so busy. She is, too. She is married and she also has a full-time job. But when Linda is left with her, she loves to talk with the child. This Linda's own mother does not do.

The baby sitter said, "This little girl—I love her dearly—is now six years old, but I have known her since she was three. Her mother leaves her with me for several hours at a time. She is so good when we are alone. If I say do this, or do that, she obeys and she is very happy to do what I ask her to do. I talk with her and I quietly explain to her what she must do and she behaves well. She likes responsibility. When her mother comes for her she doesn't want to go home.

Her mother is her servant

"One day I took her home and she changed completely when we were in the door. She told her mother she had left her chewing gum upstairs and she wanted it. I said, 'Linda, you go up and get the gum yourself!' She said, 'No, my mommy will get it for me!' She had a tantrum, stamped her foot and made such a fuss that her mother went upstairs and got the gum for her. I can't understand this way of treating children."

The mother gave Linda a sense of insecurity

What makes the difference in this child's behavior? The difference is in the way the two women communicate with her. Her mother is too busy, or too unconcerned, to explain to her daughter why she must learn to do certain things herself. She treats the girl as though she were irresponsible and probably couldn't do the things for herself. The mother gives the girl a sense of insecurity. The child resents this and takes cruel advantage of it.

The baby sitter, on the other hand, loves this little girl enough to talk with her, explain what she must do and why. She shows she is interested in Linda as an important individual. She patiently listens to the child. Her attention and her guidance communicate security and respect as well as affection. This the little girl needs.

Children feel the need for guidance

And this she will need more and more as she reaches adolescence. As one child counsellor said, "Children feel the need for guidance. They know they can't make all their own decisions. They must rely on loving adults, preferably their own parents, to direct them until they can learn self-direction and self-discipline."

The mother of two teen-agers said, "You've got to instill trust in your children if you want them to listen to you and to communicate confidently with you. They're so used to being double crossed. If you promise to do something for them, be sure to do it. They must feel they can rely on you."

Children don't learn to communicate automatically when they become twenty-one

A father of a teen-age son said, "We give our children too many things, do too much for them. At lunch today a friend asked me, 'I'm either going to send my boy to Switzerland this year or buy him a color television set. Which do you think I should do?' I said, 'Neither. If you do everything for the boy just because you can afford to, you're not doing him a favor. My own son works in a super market after high school two evenings a week and all day Saturday. He deposits his earnings in the bank every week. He also makes a little money playing in an orchestra. If I didn't encourage him to step out and work where he meets all sorts of people how would he ever learn to get along with people, to communicate with them? You don't learn this suddenly when you become twenty-one years old, you know!' "

If you have been spoiling one of your children, don't assume you have a hopeless problem child on your hands. It's never too late to start thinking of his needs and to start communicating with him in terms of these needs.

The experience of child counsellors who have worked on many difficult cases show that children react well to parental firmness if this is combined with love and affection.

How Jimmy's parents helped him when they changed their way of communicating with him

The Wallaces had a problem child because they had been over-protective with Jimmy for eleven years. But they were wise enough to change their method of communicating with this boy and he soon developed a fine character that made them proud of him.

One evening not long ago, Jimmy was sitting on a rustic fence which stretched across the lawn in front of his home. He rocked back and forth for a while, then suddenly fell backwards off the fence. He lay where he fell and started to cry. His mother and father, Mary and Ed Wallace, were sitting on the terrace not far away. Ed said, "I better go out there and pick the boy up. He might be hurt."

Mary said, "You'll do no such thing. You know very well he isn't hurt. He fell over backwards on the lawn. He's just crying as he always has whenever he wanted us to do something for him. He's eleven years old and he's still a baby. It's our fault, Ed, but in fairness to Jimmy we've got to stop it."

They agreed to stop "babying" him

Ed sank back in his chair and said, "You're right, Mary. The kid isn't hurt so let him squall. As you said, it's about time we thought of him instead of ourselves."

In a little while Jimmy picked himself up. He wasn't hurt at all but he was still crying when he walked across the terrace on his way to the house. He sobbed, "Nobody around here appreciates me. You wouldn't care if I was dead."

His mother said, "Jimmy, darling, we do appreciate you. That's why we've decided to stop treating you like a baby and treat you like a young man. We should have done this long ago. We owe you an apology and an explanation. Please go into the house and wash those childish tears out of your eyes and come back here. The three of us will have a little talk."

When she was telling me about this experience, Mary said, "Jimmy must have thought over what I said and I guess he liked it, because when he came back out, he wasn't crying. I told him, 'We should apologize for treating you like a baby so long. There are two reasons why we have done this. In the first place, you are our youngest. And in the second place you were a premature baby. You spent the first two months of your life in an incubator and when we finally brought you home from the hospital, we were so glad to have you that we began to be overly protective and overly solicitous and we have been ever since.'

They discuss what they believe he really needs

" 'As I watched you lying on your back out on the lawn crying just now, I knew you weren't hurt. You were crying simply because you wanted sympathy and attention. We decided that there was something you might want even more and that is recognition as an important member of our family. Isn't that true?'

"Jimmy said, 'I guess so.'

"His father said, 'If you stop thinking of yourself all the time and show us that you want to be an important member of this family team, maybe we'll help you get a horse for yourself just as we helped your brother and sister.' "

Mary told me, "Now Jimmy was really interested. He said, 'Gee, dad, can I have a horse of my own, all mine?'

They promise Jim a reward

"Ed said, 'Yes you can as soon as you learn to do things for yourself instead of expecting others to wait on you. You would have to take care of your horse yourself.' "

The Wallaces are not wealthy people. They have a house and barn on several acres on the outskirts of a small community. When the older children wanted horses, Ed told them to save their money. When they saved enough to pay for half the cost of a horse, he loaned them the other half. Each could have a horse if he agreed to take care of it and pay for its feed out of his allowance or out of money he earned by doing odd jobs in the community.

Ed told me, "We never had any trouble with our older kids because we taught them to do things for themselves as soon as they could walk. We didn't wait on them as we did with Jimmy."

I asked, "Ed, after that talk you and Mary had with Jimmy, did he change overnight into a cooperative member of the family team?"

Ed said, "I wish I could say he did. But I guess it isn't possible to change habits overnight. He agreed to stop being a baby principally because he began to think about something he wanted badly—his own horse. He kept after me until I agreed to go with him to a nearby stable to pick out a horse. This we did and Jimmy was a very proud young man."

I asked, "What happened?"

Ed said, "After the first week Jimmy would not take care of the horse. In the evening when he should have gone out to the stable to feed and water the horse and clean out the stall, he'd find some excuse to avoid doing this. He'd complain that he had a cold or a headache and he'd ask his older brother to do this chore for him.

Jim didn't keep his agreement

"As soon as I heard about this I had a talk with Jimmy. I said, 'Look Jim, you wanted a horse. I agreed to help you buy him on condition that you would take care of him. Is that right?' Jimmy agreed.

"I said, 'This you haven't done. You probably expect me to punish you in some way but I am not going to. You and I made an agreement. I kept my part, you haven't been keeping yours. If you don't take care of the horse as you said you would, I will take him away and sell him.'

"Jim probably didn't believe that I would do anything as drastic as that. In any event, the habit of trying to get others in the family to do things for him was so strong he slipped a few times again during the week and let the other kids feed and water his horse.

Jim's father kept his word—he took the reward away

"At the end of the week I took the horse back and sold him.
"You never saw such a startled youngster. He was so shocked when he found his horse was gone he just ran up to his room and closed the door. When he came down a little later his eyes were red. He came over to me and said, 'That was an awful thing to do. But I guess I deserved it. I'm sorry.'"

Ed said, "You're writing about communications in the home. Well I think this illustrates an important point in communicating with children. They need a feeling of security. To have this feeling of security their parents must tell them what they have to do in order to be respected and responsible members of the family. This helps them develop self-confidence and self-discipline as they grow up.

Jimmy "grew up"

"Jimmy was an entirely different boy during the next month. He listened to his mother when she spoke to him. He did what we asked him to do. He was more cooperative, argued less with his brother and sisters. He seemed to grow up, to have more stature. When I saw that this improvement continued for a month, I said to him one day, 'Jimmy, how would you like to have another horse?'

"He said, 'Gee, dad, that would be great! I think I'm ready for it now.'

He got another horse because he earned the right to have it

"We went out that Saturday and bought a beautiful chestnut mare for Jimmy. And now none of the other three horses get better care than Jim gives his mare. When we see him riding in the local horse shows with the other kids, we're glad we didn't continue to communicate with him as though he were a baby whom we'd have to protect and cater to for the rest of his life."

This experience of Mary and Ed Wallace with their youngest son illustrates several important factors in successful communication with children. First of all, as psychologists tell us, all children are born self-centered. They are little I-Landers who think in terms of "I" and "me" and "mine" until their parents teach them the advantages of thinking about others.

Secondly, when children have been spoiled by over-protective, over-solicitous parents for ten or twelve years, they don't become self-disciplined, cooperative members of the family overnight. Changing them may take a little time. But they will accept responsibility and will become self-directive if the parents explain the many advantages of this.

Finally, children appreciate parents who will talk out problems with them. One of their problems is winning the respect and approval of the rest of the family. They want and need this. They welcome help in getting it, because only when they are respected and admired by the family group do they have the feeling of security they need.

Is communication with children the most neglected area of family life?

One child counsellor said the most neglected area of family life is the unintelligent way parents talk to their children and the way they talk to each other in front of their children.

His studies of family conversations disclosed many cases where parents were constantly nagging either the children or each other. They frequently were complaining, criticizing, quarreling. He found many homes where there was an overall negative and hostile atmosphere.

Naturally the children absorb this because they often pattern their own communications after that of their parents. When a teacher told a mother her twelve-year-old son used profanity when arguing with other boys at school, the mother said, "Why, I can't understand that!" However, she knew the reason—his father and she both use that kind of language when they quarrel with each other in front of the children.

*Learn to communicate successfully
with your children*

If you want your children to grow up into well adjusted,
happy adults, use the ABC technique in your family conversations, especially with your children. Study each child, learn
to sense his individual needs and his reactions, communicate
with him in terms of his interests, and show him you are interested in him.

Give your child the individual recognition that every youngster wants. Remember the mother of the little girl who greeted
her each morning by saying, "Look who's here!" This made
her feel like an important member of the family.

Put down your newspaper, stop what you're doing when
your child wants your attention. Smile at him. Call him by
name instead of "son," "junior," or "sis." Children, too, love
the sound of their names. Show by your attitude and the way
you greet your children that they are not annoying interrup-
tions, but interesting and important to you.

Listen attentively—teach each child to listen

Give your child your attention. When he talks to you, listen
to him. Let him discuss his problems with you. Don't be too
busy to listen. Answer his questions. Ask him questions that
show you are interested in what he has to say. Teach him to
listen.

During a discussion in a University of Michigan speech as-
sembly recently it was agreed that the child taught to be an
effective "listener" is likely to become a good husband, wife,
and parent, a good congressman, or business executive—or just
a good guy to go fishing with.

*See that the tone of your voice
communicates genuine interest*

The tone of your voice means much to a child and may tell
him more than your words do. If you're having dinner in a

restaurant and your waiter sounds irritable and tense, as though he's just had an argument with someone, you don't enjoy your meal as much as you would if it were served by a considerate hostess with a soft, well-modulated, friendly voice.

See that the tone of your voice does not communicate impatience or annoyance. Let it communicate confidence and genuine interest.

To children actions often speak louder than words

Your actions tell a child much about your interest in him. Do the things that you tell him you will do even when they happen to be unpleasant to him and to you. Let him see that you consider him important enough to keep the agreements you make with him. And don't pick up your newspaper and read it while he is talking to you. Show him he is more important than your paper.

One of the most effective ways to communicate with children is by example. One couple I know have agreed that they would never under any circumstances quarrel in front of their children. When they have a difference of opinion one will suggest, "Let's discuss this later when we have more time to go into it." And the other will agree.

Hold family conferences

Another family has found that it helps to have problem solving conferences with their children. When a problem comes up (for instance, if one child wants to watch a certain program on television and another wants to watch a different program), they call a conference. During this conference the group will decide which program is to be turned on. They have found this conference approach helps promote understanding and helps minimize quarrels.

Remember the advice of the mother of the year: "Love your children with all your heart, but love them enough to discipline them."

Let's discipline ourselves to communicate successfully

It is necessary to discipline children in the sense that we must train them to take their place in the family as respected and responsible individuals. This gives them the feeling of security they need, helps them learn self-direction and self-discipline.

Perhaps it would be helpful if parents would discipline themselves to use the ABC technique for more success on the human side of family communication.

When you study each child individually and sense his needs and his reactions, when you communicate with him in terms of his interests and demonstrate your interest in him, you are sure to be more successful in getting him to listen to you, understand you and react the way you want him to. Moreover, you will help him grow up to be the type of individual who will make you proud of him.

"Talking is one of the fine arts . . . and its fluent harmonies may be spoiled by the intrusion of a single harsh note."

OLIVER WENDELL HOLMES

Chapter 8

EASE YOUR WAY THROUGH THESE
POTENTIAL STRESS POINTS AND YOU'LL
HAVE A HAPPIER FAMILY LIFE

In Chapter One we discussed the findings of Professor Meier who said, "Communications are interactions between human beings . . . At some point, probably different for each person . . . the pace of communications becomes stressful." When the stress becomes intense, we break down, blow up, or have to escape.

There are a number of potential stress points in family communications. If we don't realize that these exist, we may not understand the explosions or the heartaches we cause. Once we are aware of them, we can be careful to ease our way through the danger areas.

The potential stress points in family communications are (1) at mealtime, (2) when the husband or wife is leaving for work, or (3) returning from work, and (4) when the family is ready to go to bed. In what way are these potential stress points? Let's discuss them one by one.

Mealtime should never become "war time"

I suggest that the psychologists at the University of Michigan communication center or at some other great university study the effect mealtime conversations have on family relationships. I believe they would find that discussions around the dining room table have a much longer-lasting effect on the participants than all the committee meetings and conferences in business organizations have on those who take part in these business discussions.

Mealtime conversations should be interesting and stimulating to every member of the family. But what happens? A group of I-Landers gather around a table. Each person is leading his own life. He is interested in his own affairs. He resents interference. He voices an opinion. He is challenged. He defends himself. An argument starts. Soon the whole family may become involved.

During dinner one evening, an unusually intelligent father who saw that the conversation bouncing back and forth across the table was reaching the stressful point said, "This is beginning to sound like a United Nations debate. Let's stop it while we're still friends. In this family we should be intelligent enough to maintain a pleasant atmosphere at the table."

But how many fathers are this objective? More often the father, or perhaps the mother may be responsible for the mealtime stress by criticizing one of the children at the table. This they should never do.

A mother told her teen-age daughter, "Take your elbows off the table, dear!" The girl did. But her two brothers smiled as though they were thinking, "She doesn't know any better." The girl resented the public criticism. When her mother repeated it several times, she got up and left the table. She said to her mother, "You hate me. I know that!" and ran out of the room.

Her mother turned to her husband and said, "What am I to do? I've got to teach her some manners."

The husband replied, "Yes, dear. But not in front of the entire family. She is sensitive. So are you. We all are. And if there is one place our feelings should not be hurt, it is when we're sitting around the dinner table with the family. In the first place, this is bad for our digestion. But more important, it's darn bad for our morale, don't you think so?" His wife agreed.

Cross these subjects off the agenda for mealtime discussion

If you haven't already done this, call a family conference and get all to agree that the following subjects will never be discussed at mealtime: anything that is contentious or might start an argument, mistakes made by any member of the family, financial troubles, illness, death, or other depressing topics, household problems or worries of any sort. Also on the forbidden list should be fault finding, teasing, criticism or anything that might be discourteous or unkind.

Choose pleasant topics for mealtime discussion

Some families maintain silence at the table. In my opinion, this is a mistake, because mealtime can be one of the most pleasant opportunities for constructive family communications.

What should a family discuss? This depends on the interest of the group. And it depends, too, on the age and number of children. In one family where there are three children from three to six, the father and mother have decided to talk only about what interests the children. They do not believe that children "should be seen and not heard" at the dinner table. They encourage their daughter and their two sons to talk about anything that interests them and the parents join in the conversation. The children feel that they are respected as important individuals and the father and mother are rewarded by seeing how the thinking ability of their flock is developing.

In another family the wife feeds the children first at one meal every day so she can have an uninterrupted discussion with her husband. The children are teen-agers and they respect their parents' desire for adult talk.

Another family is interested in travel and languages. The

parents and the children are having fun learning a number of foreign languages. They want to be able to communicate with the people in the countries they visit. At mealtime they talk only in the language they are studying that particular day—and only about the country or countries in which that language is spoken. This is fun for them all. And they do not have to wonder whether any member of the family isn't listening or trying to understand. Remember, each of us listens when he *wants* to listen!

Other topics for mealtime conversation might be any one of the following, depending on the interest of the various members of the family: books, magazine articles, the theater, art, philosophy, national or international affairs, your United States Senators or Representatives, the officials of your state and community and their work, church affairs, people you know, relatives and friends, television or radio programs, so many things that are constructive and could be interesting to everyone.

One family decided to exact a penalty from the one who starts a discussion of anything negative or contentious during mealtime. The guilty one puts ten cents in a piggy bank. The piggy bank was named "Good Time Charlie." When it is full, it is opened and the accumulated "loot" is used to finance a good time for the whole family, usually a dinner out and a movie.

Start a "Good Time Charlie" in your family if you wish. It sounds as though it could be fun. But, in any event, decide to ease your way through one of the principal stress points in family communications—meal time—by establishing a rule that only pleasant, constructive conversation will be permitted at your table.

Make leaving the house so pleasant your
husband looks forward to returning

Dr. Gerald Gordon, chief psychiatrist of E. I. du Pont de Nemours & Company said that a large proportion of the stress ailments that are blamed on job pressures actually originate in a man's private life, and particularly in family relationships. One of the chief points of potential stress is the moment a husband leaves home to go to work. What happens at this time?

In some homes, the wife might follow her husband to the door and continue the argument that started at breakfast. Or she may remind him of everything she wants him to do for her during the day. One wife told her husband as he was leaving for work, "Remember to mail the letters I gave you and drop the bag of wash off at the laundry and stop in at the grocer's on the way home and pick up the things I need and have that noisy muffler on the car fixed. Drive carefully. It's raining today, so be particularly careful!"

A husband whose wife told him explicitly what to do as he left for work said, "I wonder how I ever learned to walk before I met you!"

Some women writers who advise other women how to live with a husband tell their readers that men like to be mothered. Perhaps the writers are married to this type of man. Take my word for it, girls, such husbands are in the minority. Chances are your man merely wants you to treat him the way you would want to be treated if your positions were reversed—as an intelligent adult who is respected by his partner.

When he is about to leave for work, send him away feeling that you respect him and consider him important to you. Show him that you are really fond of him. Forget the chores at this time. If you have things you want him to do, give him a list of them earlier, perhaps just after breakfast.

If he puts the list in his pocket, don't remind him of it when he is leaving. Give him credit for being able to remember it.

If he forgets, what difference does it make? You'd rather be happy than have cream in your coffee the next day, wouldn't you? And you'd rather have a husband who leaves you thinking you're the most wonderful girl in the world than one who cusses and grumbles all the way to work and wonders how he ever tangled up with an inconsiderate shrew.

Ease your way pleasantly through the going-to-work time of potential stress. Send friend husband on his way feeling cheerful and confident and you'll be rewarded by having a healthier, happier and more successful husband.

Make it a pleasure to come home

Some wives start criticizing their husbands even before the men walk into the house. While her husband was getting out of the car in the driveway, one wife came to the door and said, "I'll bet you forgot to pick up my dress at the cleaner's!" When he reached into the back of the car and brought out the dress, she said, "Oh, this time you didn't forget!" She walked down the steps to meet her husband and she said, "Give me the dress and take in that garden hose curled up on the front lawn before somebody breaks his neck. You left it there last night!" The husband who told me about this incident said he wondered why he bothered to come home.

Other wives may greet their husbands with the sad story of all the trouble they had getting the children to behave, or they may tell him about all the work they did during the day and the trouble they had with the maid or the baby-sitter. Of course, a husband wants to hear about these things. But not as soon as he walks in the door. Perhaps he has had a bad day himself and he, too, needs a sympathetic ear.

A considerate wife makes coming home a pleasure for her husband. She knows he may be tired, worn out by the frustrations and pressures of his work. She realizes that if she were in his place she would want peace and quiet, someone to talk to and relax with. So she plans to make homecoming one of her husband's most pleasant experiences. Such thoughtful wives have little trouble getting their husbands to listen to them and understand them.

Have a bedtime harmony hour

The final potential period of stress is the hour before the

family goes to bed. In my book, *Let's Not Worry, Let's Not Fuss—Let's Just Be Glad We're Us,* I asked, "Have you ever tried to go to bed with all your clothes on?" And I said, "You wouldn't sleep very well, would you? Well, it's just as silly to go to bed with the hurt feelings, anxieties, worries or other troubles of the day. Put them all out of your mind when you go to bed and you'll sleep like a baby."

In some families, people quarrel right up to the time they go to bed, even argue back and forth while they are in bed. They try to go to sleep but they can't sleep because they're upset. They're angry, hurt, resentful. This is bad, particularly bad for family communications. When each partner stews over what he thinks is the other's unreasonableness his resentment can turn to bitterness and even to hate. This makes him unwilling to try to understand the other's point of view.

To avoid this unpleasant experience one couple agreed early in their married life that they would never go to bed angry with each other. No matter how severe the strain might seem, they would make up before going to bed.

This has been difficult to do at times. A husband and wife do not follow the Marquis of Queensbury rules when they slug each other with verbal punches. There is no time keeper to ring a bell at the end of each round and stop the fight at the end of ten or fifteen rounds. There is no referee to award the bout to one or the other or call it a draw. Some family quarrels go on for days.

Not in this couple's home, however. They always kiss each other good night. They have kept their agreement to make up before going to bed, and they tell me this has helped them maintain a harmonious relationship.

You'll sleep better and live longer

Why wait until you're ready for bed to "make up" any differences? Why wouldn't it be better judgment to have a "harmony hour"? For one hour before bed time, no arguments, no criticism, no contentiousness, no complaints. Only constructive, considerate discussions—just friendly harmony! If you do not have this policy in your family, try it. You'll sleep better and live longer.

Remember the potential stress points we have discussed in this chapter. You're forewarned! Ease your way through them and you'll communicate more successfully and have a happier family life.

"Some men move through life as a band of music moves down a thoroughfare flinging out melody and harmony through the air to everyone far and near who listens."

HENRY WARD BEECHER

Chapter 9

YOU'LL HAVE MANY MORE FRIENDS EAGER TO HEAR ANYTHING YOU HAVE TO SAY

Cy Sterling is a very good friend of mine—and of hundreds of other people all over the world. Seeing him is a delightful experience. I don't know of anyone who has met Cy who doesn't like him. Somehow you become more cheerful, you feel better when he walks into the room. Your tension eases. You relax. You feel that here is one person who really is a friend!

Cy is a colonel in the United States Marine Corps. Although his tours of duty have taken him all over the world and there are many stories he could tell about the colorful places he has seen, he never talks about himself or what he has done—unless you ask him to. When you meet him, his first thought is about you. His greeting is something like this, "It's so good to see you! What have you been doing since I saw you last?"

If you happen to say you haven't been doing much of anything, he'll say, "Oh, come on now, you've been doing a lot of interesting things. Tell me about some of them."

138 MAKE YOUR FRIENDS EAGER TO LISTEN

You're "on stage"

What does this greeting do to you? It puts you up on the stage. The spotlight is on you. And Cy is your audience. He smiles in anticipation of what you are going to say. You know he is interested in you. Of course, you like him.

Do you see why he has so many friends? He listens. He shows he is interested in the people he meets. He talks to them in terms of their own interests. He uses the ABC Human Side of Communication technique. He probably does this unconsciously, as many popular people do, but nevertheless he does use it and he has hundreds of friends.

When you study the people you know in order to sense their needs and their reactions, what is the first thing you find that they need?

Most of us need someone who will listen to us

You find that one of their most serious needs is for someone to listen to them, to show he really is interested in hearing how they feel, how they think, what they have been doing.

This need is so widespread it was made the subject of a book called *The Listener* * which quickly became a best seller. In this book, the author, Taylor Caldwell, told how desperate some of us become when we can find no one who will listen to us. She reported a number of cases where men and women saved their sanity, remade their lives, just because they found someone who would listen to them, even though that someone did not say a word, could not say a word in reply.

We know our friends need someone who will listen to them, but what do we often do? We're probably I-Landers so we start talking about ourselves and the things that concern us. We assume the other person is interested in us. Perhaps he is gracious enough to listen, so we decide he really likes us. Ah, this is a friend!

---

* Published by Doubleday, New York.

When we meet him again we are inclined to bring him up-to-date on everything that has happened to us which we think might be worth telling. We may not wonder whether he wants to hear all this. At times we may be so happy to have someone to talk to that we do not give our friend an opportunity to tell us some of the things he may want to discuss.

When we bore our friends, we sometimes lose them

When some of those we thought of as friends haven't been in touch with us for a long time, we sometimes say, "I wonder what happened to them? We used to be good friends, but now we seldom see each other." Perhaps we bore them by our I-Lander monologues, by interrupting them, by showing our sole interest was in ourselves.

Mary Caldwell and Bill Jackson were close friends for seven years. They went everywhere together. Mary told her sister, "I'm crazy about Bill. He's the most charming man I've ever met. You know I'm a chatterbox. I probably was vaccinated with a phonograph needle. But Bill always listens to me. He seems interested in everything I say."

We all expected Bill to marry Mary. But he didn't. He married another girl, Sarah Stein. Sarah wasn't as attractive as Mary. But Sarah seldom talked about herself unless Bill asked her about something she had done. She was interested in Bill and evidently loved to listen to him.

Mary said Bill was charming because he always was willing to listen to her; Sarah, on the other hand, found Bill an interesting person and she encouraged him to express his own opinions about business, national affairs, family life, and everything else she thought might interest him.

Mary wore out her audience

Mary loved having the spotlight turned on herself. She monopolized the center of the stage. To her, Bill was a good audience. Her "play," which we might call "The Life and

Private Interests of Mary," had a long run—over seven years. However, it finally wore out its audience appeal.

Soliloquies are seldom popular

Perhaps Shakespeare was right when he said, "All the world's a stage and all the men and women merely players." If we are players on the world stage, certainly all of us appreciate an enthusiastic audience.

We seldom like anyone who hogs the spotlight and strides back and forth across the stage delivering a soliloquy while he assumes that we will sit out front entranced by every word he speaks.

Do you want to have many more friends, friends who are eager to hear anything you have to say? If your answer is, "Yes," do this one thing and you'll be as popular as you ever hoped to be: give your friends the center spot on the stage before you grab the spotlight yourself.

Let your friends enjoy the spotlight when they're with you

Put the spotlight on them. Show them that you are interested in them. Show them that you are an appreciative audience. Never interrupt them. When they're telling a story don't look impatient as though you can't wait to jump in with one of your own.

Wait until they give you your cue before you step up to the stage. When you get your cue, they'll be ready to listen to you and listen favorably to everything you have to say.

Giving our friends the stage isn't easy. Most of us are I-Landers. We want others to be interested in us. We prefer to talk about ourselves and our own interests. When I was riding across town in New York the other day, I asked the taxi driver, "Do you have any trouble getting people to listen to you and understand you?" He said, "Do I? Even your own friends don't listen to you these days. Everyone is so self-centered! It seems the only way you can get another person's attention is to talk about him. If you talk about him for two or three minutes, his mind will come down out of the clouds and he'll start being interested in what you have to say."

Perhaps this is a cynical observation. However, it is somewhat accurate because we seem to be living in a world of I-Landers. Most of the I-Landers are fine people. They just happen to be interested primarily in themselves. They become fond of someone else only when they see that he is interested in them.

When they see that another person is interested only in himself, they soon find him dull and unattractive and they see him only when they have to. Sometimes they lose interest in seven minutes, sometimes in seven years.

If you could keep all the friends you ever made just think how many you'd have!

Some of us probably blunder through life making and losing friends. Perhaps it never occurs to us to wonder why we lose contact with those who might have been dear friends. Then again we might be fortunate enough to have a flash of awareness and change our methods of communicating before it is too late.

Such a flash of awareness came to Fred Burke some time ago. After living in apartments or rented houses for many years, he and his wife Sally bought a home in California. They had looked for one for five or six years. Naturally when they found the type of place for which they had been looking, a red wood ranch house on a wooded hill overlooking the Pacific Ocean, they were happy about it. They took photographs, as many other families no doubt do when they move into "the home of their dreams."

A few months later they flew to New York to see some of the friends they hadn't seen for some time. Fred told me that a couple they like very much invited them to a cocktail party.

Several other friends were there. When they arrived Fred said he hardly waited to remove his coat and hat and exchange the usual greetings before he took out the photographs of the new house. He said, "Here are some pictures of the new home we bought." Fred was sort of shocked when his host said, "Oh, let's not start looking at photographs so early. Put them away and we'll look at them later. We've seen houses before."

Fred said, "Were our friends glad to see the photos we had brought? They were not! There were six or eight people in this group we hadn't seen for some time. Collectively they had much more to tell us than we had to tell them. We shouldn't have assumed that our adventure in finding a pleasant home would be as exciting to them as it was to us. We put the photographs away and didn't take them out again all evening.

When you listen, they love you

"As a matter of fact," Fred said, "no one inquired about the photographs. Each was so busy helping us catch up on the news about his family, his job and his experiences that we felt that we had never moved away from New York. Our visit became a pleasant experience. We realized that friends love you most when you listen to them and are interested in them. But they do not want to be slugged into listening (or appearing to listen) to you as you tell about the things that interest you."

The next day Fred said he and Sally visited another group of friends. He said, "This time we did not offer to show the photographs. We did not talk about ourselves or our new home. We talked about our friends and their families and their interests.

"Before long one of them said, 'Say, you bought a house in California, didn't you?'

"I said, 'Yes, but that was some months ago.'

"The friend asked, 'What's it like? Haven't you taken any pictures of it?'

"I said, 'Yes, we have a few pictures. Some relatives wanted to see what it looked like so we took a few snapshots but they don't amount to much.'

"Several of the friends in the group said almost together, 'Let's see them! We'd like to see what your new house looks like.' We had listened to them. Now they were ready and willing to listen to us."

They waited for their "cue"

What made the difference in the interest that these two groups showed? You know the answer. Most of the individuals in each of the groups were interested in talking about themselves. Just as you and I are.

In the first case Fred started to talk about his interests before he gave his friends a chance to tell all the important things that had happened to them since Fred and Sally saw them last.

Fred tried to take the floor before he was invited. This annoyed his audience, so his "audience" refused to listen. In the second case, Fred listened first, waited for his cue and then he had a receptive audience.

Perhaps it's natural to want to talk about yourself. You live with yourself 24 hours a day. What could be more fascinating to you than your own thoughts, your own experiences? When you meet someone who shows he is interested in you, immediately you have something in common—a common interest in you! So you like him. You want him to be your friend. How can you make this person you like become your friend?

The friendship of another individual is one of the most delightful experiences anyone can have. This is worth thinking about. To earn the friendship of the people you like and to make their friendship grow stronger, use the ABC technique for success on the human side of communications.

Show you're interested in him

When you study each friend so you can sense his needs and his reactions, you will see that one of his principal needs is to know that you are interested in him—interested enough to let him have the center of the stage with you as an appreciative audience.

So give him your complete and sincere attention before you demand his attention. Listen to him with all your being before you ask him to listen to you.

For instance, when you want to talk about your bowling score, first ask him about his bowling score. Let him tell you how well he is doing lately. Before long he will be satisfied and pleased to see your interest in him, and he will ask you to tell him how well you have been bowling. This is your "cue." He's ready to listen to you.

If he tells you about a book he has read, and tells you he thinks it might be one you'd like to read, buy a copy, or get one from the library. Tell him you did this. He'll know you really did listen to him and you were sincere when you seemed interested. Let your friend see that you respect his recommendations and he'll be more interested in listening to yours.

When you come back from a trip and have movies of your pleasant experiences, don't call a friend and say, "Come on over and let us show you the movies of all the fun we had." If he's visited the same places, call him and say, "You've seen all these places. Why don't you come over and we'll compare notes. Tell us whether your experiences were similar to the ones we had when we visited the places you will see in the movies we took."

If your friend hasn't visited the places you've seen, you might say, "You probably will be going to these places one of these days, so why don't you come over and look at the scenes we photographed. Perhaps they will give you some ideas about trips that you will want to take or are planning right now." In other words, put your friend up there on the stage, talk about your experiences in terms of your friend's interests. You will demonstrate your interest in him and he will want to listen to you.

Ask his opinion

When you feel inclined to tell your friend about your opinion of world affairs, the national government, business conditions, or anything else, first ask his opinion. When he gives it to you, listen attentively. If it doesn't happen to agree with yours, don't argue with him. Just tell him what you think about the situation.

But always avoid making an emphatic statement such as, "This is the way it is!" A statement of this sort may suggest to him that you believe you are right and he is wrong. Don't give him the impression that you want to be the star of the discussion and he doesn't count. Avoid this possibility by making frequent use of the words, "In my opinion." For instance, say, "In my opinion, this is the way the situation is." In this way you acknowledge the fact that he, too, is entitled to an opinion. And he may be right.

Help each friend to feel important to you. Let him know he will always be a star on your stage. Ask his opinion. Listen to him. Encourage him to talk about his interests.

Incidentally, the word "friend" comes from the Anglo-Saxon verb "frēon" meaning to love. Love your friends enough to listen to them and they'll love you dearly.

There is no more rewarding place to use the ABC technique of successful communication than in the development and nourishment of friendship. Instead of taking your friends for granted, study them, learn to sense their needs, and their reactions.

Talk to them in terms of their own interests.

Show them that you are interested in them by keeping them in the spotlight on your stage and you will never have any trouble getting them to listen to you and understand you. They will *want* to. Why? Because they will consider you one of the most charming and most interesting persons they know.

PART III

SUCCESSFUL COMMUNICATION
AT WORK

"He that ruleth his speech is better than he that taketh a city."

KING SOLOMON

Chapter 10

WAS DISRAELI RIGHT WHEN HE SAID,
"WITH WORDS WE GOVERN MEN"?

During a recent workshop seminar on business communications, one of the participants, Paul Kelly, said, "It sure is necessary to know how to communicate with others if you're going to enjoy your work and get anywhere. For instance, I've been working for the same boss nearly ten years. I know how to communicate with him. So I enjoy working for him and I get anything I want from him. Others who approach him the wrong way think he's tough, but he isn't if you handle him right."

One of the other workshop participants, Joe Bates, asked, "Why do you have to 'handle' your boss right? I don't try to do this. I think my work should speak for itself. I don't believe in soft soaping the boss."

Paul asked, "Do you have any trouble with your boss, any major differences of opinion?"

Joe said, "Yes. He doesn't seem to understand some of my problems. And often I feel he isn't in sympathy with what I'm trying to do. But that's his fault. I keep him informed in conferences and through reports. But like everyone else, he's so busy he probably doesn't remember half what he hears and perhaps he doesn't have time to read all the reports he gets."

Whose fault is it when the boss doesn't understand you?

Paul said, "The fact that he doesn't understand some of the things you tell him could be your fault, you know. There are ways to make your boss or anyone else understand you and cooperate with you. This isn't always easy, but it can be done if you talk to him in the right way. I'm not suggesting that you soft soap the guy. I'm saying I've found it pays to study my boss so I can understand him and the job that he's trying to do. I find when I do this, and then do what we're discussing in this workshop—communicate with my boss in terms of his interests —I get along with him fine.

There must be many Joe Bates in the business world. In Chapter One we discussed a study of communications in business made by University of Michigan psychologists. You remember what they found—that the boss seldom knew what his junior executive's problems were. Frequently the two men did not even agree on what the assistant was supposed to be doing! In only 6 per cent of the cases were the two men in complete agreement about the junior executive's problems.

How well are you communicating with the people with whom you work, with your superiors and those who work for you? Are you a Joe Bates, or a Paul Kelly who believes in learning how to understand the people with whom he works in order to communicate with them successfully and make his own work more pleasant and rewarding?

If you wish to be sure you are getting through to others at work when you talk or write to them, use the same ABC technique we have been discussing for successful communication at home.

First, study the other person, learn to sense his needs and his reactions. Then, communicate with him in terms of his own interests. And show him you are interested in him.

What do you learn when you study the other people around you? Usually you find they're not automatically interested in you. They're interested in themselves. Most of them are I-Landers. While they are working, they're thinking about their success, their profit, their security.

How do you get cooperation?

You want their cooperation. In some cases you need this if you are going to enjoy your own work and be successful at it. So what must you do? You must keep in your mind the other fellow's point of view. You must talk to him in terms of what he wants. When you ignore him, refuse to consider his ideas, you can get into trouble.

Even otherwise intelligent people can lose opportunities for advancement or even lose their jobs by ignoring the point of view of people with whom they work. For instance, there is a brilliant man who was asked to resign from a good job recently. Few other men could do his work as well. But he wasn't willing to consider the ideas of a new manager. He had been chosen tentatively as this new man's assistant, and this would have given him a bigger salary, but he missed this chance and also lost his job, even though he had worked for the organization nearly ten years.

He wouldn't try to understand his boss's point of view

Two divisions of the company were merged. One of the division managers was made head of the merged organization. He wanted to make some changes in the operations of the company that would increase sales and cut costs. He needed an assistant to handle the details for him. The man he considered for the job had a record for conscientious and efficient work. He told this man about his plans and his proposed program. The man said flatly, "It won't work. We've been doing things the same way for years. We've been successful. Why change?"

The new manager asked, "Aren't you at least willing to explore the possibility of developing these plans further in order to see whether there would be an improvement?"

The man said, "No. We would be foolish to interfere with something that is successful. Why try anything else?"

He not only did not get the job, but he was asked to resign a short time later. He wasn't willing to try to understand the new boss or communicate with him in terms of the things that interested him.

Another man was hired as assistant manager. The new man doesn't have the other's experience or brains, but he knows how to communicate successfully. When his boss says, "This is the way we should improve our production methods. Do you think it will work?" the new man replied, "This sounds good to me. I don't see why it won't work. Let's try it on a small run and compare the results. If we can get a better product and save money, we sure are going to do it!"

Do you see why he got the job? He showed he was willing to try to understand his boss and help the boss get the improved profit he was hoping for. He communicated successfully.

Why people fail or make a success of their jobs

This true story of the effect their communications had on the success of two men is an example of what C. E. Duggan, President of Comidex Corporation, Mamaroneck, New York, was referring to when he said, "Other people make up the common denominator in all business activity. Time after time it is confirmed that only 10 per cent of the failures can't do the work, while 90 per cent have not developed the art of successfully communicating with people."

Evidently Disraeli was right when he said, "With words we govern men." The words we use and the way we use them can determine how well we influence the thoughts and actions of those with whom we come in contact.

To select the right words and use them effectively, it is essential that we know as much as possible about the one with whom we wish to communicate. So we study him. We ask questions. And we listen.

Studies indicate that many people in supervisory positions do not do this. They don't bother to study each individual who works for them. Perhaps some have the old-fashioned notion that the proper way to "handle" people is simply to tell them what to do and expect them to do it. But people are not machines. You can't press a button and get the results you want. You get the best results when you communicate with them in a friendly, understanding way and make them want to give you the cooperation you need.

How to "handle" people

There have been many discussions in business publications about the ways to "handle" people. It has been said that a successful supervisor is one who knows how to "handle" people. In his book *The Practice of Management* * Peter Drucker said, "The successful manager does not 'handle' people; he motivates, guides, and organizes people to do their own work. His tool—his only tool—to do all this is the spoken or written word or the language of numbers.

"No matter whether the manager's job is engineering, accounting, or selling, his effectiveness depends on his ability to listen and to read, on his ability to speak and to write. He needs skill in getting his thinking across to other people as well as skill in finding out what other people are after."

Yes, we need skill in getting our thinking across to other people and skill in finding out what other people are after. Communication, to be effective, must be two-way. We must learn what others want, so we can talk to them in terms of their own interests.

* Harper & Brothers, New York.

Take General Marshall's advice

When General George Marshall was Chief of Staff during World War II, it was his practice to call in his generals for a conference before he sent them overseas. He gave them this advice: (1) listen to the other person's story, (2) don't get mad, and (3) let others tell their stories first.

That is good advice to follow when you are endeavoring to learn the other person's point of view so you can communicate with him in a way that will make him *want* to listen to you.

Study the other person; learn to sense his needs and his reactions

Everyone with whom you work is a distinctive individual. Get to know him. Try to understand him. Talk the language he wants to hear. Become one of those rare people who says the right thing at the right time. Everybody likes them and co-operates with them.

In the next two chapters we will discuss the specific techniques that can help you make the people with whom you work understand you and gladly cooperate with you. Use these techniques and you may find you enjoy your work more and achieve all the success you'd like to have.

"Surely human affairs would be far happier if the power in men to be silent were the same as that to speak. But experience more than sufficiently teaches that men govern nothing with more difficulty than their tongues."

BARUCH SPINOZA

Chapter 11

TO BE MORE SUCCESSFUL IN YOUR
WORK, TALK THE LANGUAGE EVERYONE
WANTS TO HEAR

When he stepped up to the microphone to address a
convention of business executives, a management consultant
started to speak in Spanish. The men and women in his audience looked bewildered. He stopped and said, "Most of you
probably didn't understand a word I just said. Why? Because I
didn't speak your language."

He went on to point out that studies show a high percentage
of business communications are failures because each person
usually talks in terms of his own interest. This is a "language"
that may not interest others, therefore, they often do not listen
or try to understand.

The buyer wasn't listening

For instance, a salesman called on a prospective buyer and
said, "I was in the neighborhood and thought I'd drop in. I
sure would like to get some of your business." This didn't communicate a thing to the prospect whose mind was cruising at
400 to 500 words a minute over the requisitions on his desk. He

sent the salesman on his way and wondered why he ever agreed to see him in the first place.

The purchasing agent of a large corporation told me that some salesmen actually come in, talk for ten or fifteen minutes about themselves or about the politics or baseball that happens to interest them, and leave without telling the purchasing man what they're trying to sell or even the name of the firm they represent!

These men get results

Yet many salesmen have learned the technique of asking questions to learn what the individual prospect's interests are. By listening to the prospect tell what he needs, they can talk to him in terms of his own interests. These salesmen are the ones who get most of the orders.

Personnel men say that many people applying for work merely bring in a resumé, say they'd like to get a job and immediately ask about the salary, the fringe benefits, vacation, insurance, and other things that interest them.

Learn what the other person needs

Rarely does someone offer to discuss what he might do for the employer. Even more unusual is the applicant who asks questions to learn what is needed so he can determine whether he would be profitable to the firm that might employ him.

A small town copywriter who had never worked in a big city advertising agency answered an ad. A large agency needed a writer. Dozens applied. The small town young man did not bring the usual résumé. He asked, "Just what do you need? I'd like to see whether I would be the right man for you."

He talked the right language

The executive interviewing the applicants answered the young copywriter's questions, but explained he wanted a writer with big city experience. The young man went back to his hotel, wrote a letter to the agency executive in which he said, "Putting myself in your place and looking at this from your side of the desk, it seems you need . . ." and he discussed the agency's needs and told how he could fill them. He got the job, The man who hired him said, "We're glad to find someone who looks at our needs from our side of the desk."

It seems that not too many of us talk the language everyone wants to hear. Why? Because most of us are I-Landers and we mostly are interested in ourselves and in expressing our thoughts in our own way. This can get us into trouble.

The wrong language causes trouble

Paul Pigors of the Massachusetts Institute of Technology told of his experience with an old line foreman in a company in Springfield, Massachusetts. This foreman was causing a lot of trouble. He was a favorite target of union grievances. "But oddly enough," Paul said, "whenever we had an interview with him, he would give all the right answers. He would assert, 'Sure, cooperation is preferable to enforcement by discipline or threat of punishment.' Naturally we used to wonder what his trouble was.

"Finally, it occurred to me that there was a little semantic difficulty there. So I asked him one day. 'Exactly what do you mean by cooperation?'

" 'What do I mean?' he exploded, 'I mean do as I say and be damn quick about it!' Well, with that definition, it was easy to understand why he was the source of so many complaints."

Writing about situations such as this in *Personnel Magazine,* Paul Pigors said, "Everybody realizes it isn't enough to get obedience and compliance; you must get *voluntary coopera-tion.* Otherwise you have nothing but low-level coordination and the continuous problem of having to enforce minimum standards.

Antagonistic cooperation vs. voluntary cooperation

"The German philosopher Kant brought this out years ago when he differentiated between what he called *antagonistic cooperation* and *voluntary cooperation*. By antagonistic cooperation, he meant the kind a man gives because he needs the pay or the job. He cooperates because he has to, not because he really wants to.

"Most of the cooperation we get in industry today is of the antagonistic type. The people just work there; they are hired out, and somebody watches them. They do whatever is necessary, but that isn't enough. We want to get voluntary cooperation in which they themselves will do what is needed."

How to get voluntary cooperation

How can we get voluntary cooperation? Not by ordering another person to do something. Not by telling him how much we want him to do it, how much it would mean to us. This would be a foreign "I-Lander language" that could mean little to our listener. It might result only in antagonistic cooperation given because the other person thinks he has to give it to keep his job. To get voluntary cooperation, we must talk to others in terms of their own interests.

They're probably I-Landers, too. But they want to hear you talk to them in their own "I-Lander language"—not in yours. They want you to be interested in their point of view, not just your own.

Study him—listen to him

How do you learn the other person's point of view, his interests? By studying him and endeavoring to sense his needs and his reactions. And by listening to him so you can learn how to talk to him in a way that will make him *want* to listen to you, understand you and react the way you want him to.

Ask questions that encourage others
to tell you their point of view

In each supervisor's office in one large organization is this sign: "WHAT DO YOU RECOMMEND?" When I asked a department head the purpose of the signs, he said, "From time to time employees come in with problems and ask the supervisor how to solve them. Instead of giving a quick answer, the supervisor points to that little sign. He invites the one with the problem to sit down and tell how he thinks it can be solved. This is appreciated. Everyone welcomes the chance to give his point of view. And frequently the employee's ideas about the solution of his own problem are the best ones we could find. But the main thing is—we listen to him. This he appreciates."

In a recent roundtable discussion on communications, a group of training directors agreed that failure to listen is probably the predominant reason for poor communication.

Become a better listener

The need to listen to others in order to determine how to communicate with them effectively is so great that seminars are now being conducted on listening.

"Good!" you might say. "Now some of the dopes I have to talk to may learn how to listen to me." Yes, they may, but this will do you little good, unless you talk to them in terms of their own interests. Remember, they may learn "how" to listen, but no one can make them listen unless they *want* to!

Ask questions—and listen

Many organizations are hiring experts to conduct surveys among employees to learn what interests them. These surveys usually involve asking a few simple questions and then listening to the workers and noting their gripes and their suggestions.

What do these programs of listening disclose? Principally that management language often means little to employees. Why? Because too often people in management talk about everything from their own point of view instead of the employees'!

For instance, when management wants to urge employees to give a full day's work for a full day's pay, someone might address this message to employees: "The productivity of this organization must be increased. Let's all work harder to increase production."

*It isn't easy to get others to understand you
unless you talk in terms that interest them*

When a cross section of employees were asked what a statement of that type would mean to them, 58 per cent said it meant that management proposed a speed-up program, 16 per cent said, "We're already breaking our necks," and many of the others said, "That's the same old boloney!"

The words "productivity" and "increase production" are management language. When you use words such as these you do not speak to the workers in terms they recognize as significant to them.

Johns Manville Corporation has conducted a work improvement program which does talk in terms of the worker's point of view. It is called a "Work Smarter" program. The slogan is "Work Smarter, Not Harder." This is something that rings a bell with employers. This is a language to which they want to listen and can easily understand.

You can learn how to communicate more successfully

Do you listen to those with whom you work? Do you listen with an open mind to learn the point of view of those around you, to learn what interests them? If you do, you'll know how to communicate with them more successfully.

Listening to others is not an art that everyone understands. Notice the people in the next conference or discussion group you attend. You'll see some that jump to conclusions quickly, interrupt before another person finishes talking, others who merely look for facts that bolster their own points of view, some who seek information that helps refute their opponents. This is superficial listening, listening that is little help in communicating effectively.

When you listen and show that you want to hear what another person has to say, you learn his point of view. You see how he reacts to yours. You learn how to communicate with him. Also, you make him more inclined to *want* to listen to you.

Listening paid

A company which did not have a good labor record and for more than ten years was not able to complete the annual negotiations for a new union contract in the 60 days allowed, this past year needed only two weeks for collective bargaining. Why? Because during the past year it has held a series of meetings between foremen and shop stewards in which the foremen listened to the stewards' gripes and their suggestions.

The stewards and the union agent liked the idea so much they suggested meetings be held to discuss any possible conflicts before the annual contract negotiations started. Management listened to the representatives of their workers. And these representatives were more interested in hearing what management had to say.

How to find the key to successful communication

To learn to talk to others with whom you work in the language they want to hear, cultivate the habit of listening to them. For instance, when someone comes to your office for a meeting, instead of going through the papers on your desk while he is talking to you, sit still for a few minutes and listen to him. You'll find the key to communicating successfully with him.

And the art of "listening" should be used when you receive a written communication from another person. When you receive a memo or a report from someone, don't just write across the top of it, "See me Monday at ten o'clock about this," and send it back.

What happens when you don't show that you "listened"

When it reaches his office, his secretary may say to him, "Look, Bill, you worked for hours on this report. You took it home and worked on it at home and when you brought it back I typed it so carefully it looked like a work of art. But what do we get? It comes back with a note, "See me Monday at ten o'clock." Probably the big so-and-so didn't even read it!"

So this man develops a belligerent state of mind, just as the woman did who waited for her husband on a street corner. She was early, but she was peeved when she saw that her husband wasn't there. She began to think he'd probably be late. And the weather man had predicted rain! She had brought her umbrella, but she thought she'd probably be soaked waiting on that exposed corner.

As she waited, she began to wonder how late her husband would be. Perhaps he might be ten minutes late, maybe he'd even be fifteen minutes late. Maybe he stopped in somewhere to have a drink with some friends and perhaps he'd forget the appointment altogether!

Well, if he did, she would brain him! She became angrier and angrier as she thought of standing there, perhaps in a downpour, while her inconsiderate husband kept her waiting for him.

Finally, he came, he happened to be on time, but she walloped him with the umbrella anyway, because she had worked herself up to that state. You no doubt remember hearing this story.

Tell him you "listened"

Well, a person who receives a note across a report or memo, "See me Monday morning at ten o'clock," can develop a state of mind much like that of the angry wife. He doesn't know what to expect. He doesn't know whether you've even read his communication, whether you "listened" to him.

So, instead of communicating in terms of your own interest —"See me . . ." and having him come to your office in a belligerent state ready to prove he's right about the things he said in the report which he's almost sure you didn't read, just add a few more words to the note you write across the corner of that report before you send it back to him. Write, "Bill, I read this."

If you can't agree with it say, "Bill, I read this. I may not be able to agree with it, but let's discuss it Monday morning at ten o'clock." Or, if it is something that you like, say, "Bill, I read this. It sounds good. Let's discuss it Monday morning at ten o'clock."

Then his girl will come into his office with a big smile and she'll say, "Look, he read it! He's ready to discuss it."

You've "listened" to him—so he'll be ready to listen to you and he'll *want* to listen to your ideas.

As one communication expert put it, understanding, loyalty, and enthusiastic cooperation do not come solely from a dissemination of clearly expressed factual information. They come, to a great extent, from an employee's awareness that he can talk man to man with his superior and his superior will listen to him and welcome his ideas.

They'll want to listen to you!

Listen to those with whom you work. Learn what interests them, so you can talk to them in terms of their own interests. When you do, you will find that they are much more likely to *want* to listen to you and react the way you want them to. You see, you will be talking the language everyone wants to hear.

"We wander through life in a semi-darkness in which none of us can distinguish exactly the features of his neighbor; only from time to time, through some experience that we have with our companion, or through some remark that he passes, he stands for a moment close to us, as though illumined by a flash of lightning."

ALBERT SCHWEITZER

Chapter 12

FOLLOW LORD CHESTERFIELD'S ADVICE
AND PEOPLE WILL BE INCLINED TO LISTEN
FAVORABLY TO WHAT YOU HAVE TO SAY

When Larry Rogers met me at the Sheraton Hotel for lunch the other day he said, "I need a drink. I'm so damn angry right now I feel like going back to the office this afternoon and turning in my resignation after seven years with the organization."

I hadn't heard Larry speak this way before. He usually is a pleasant, even-tempered person. He is the assistant to one of the vice presidents of a large national organization. I asked him, "What makes you feel this way?"

He said, "Let's get a table, order that drink and I'll tell you all about it."

When we were seated at the table, Larry said, "You know my boss. He's a charming person. You would think it would be a pleasure to work for him. But it isn't. I do most of the work and he takes all the credit.

"I even write his speeches. As I was leaving the office just now to meet you, he walked out with me. The president of our outfit was standing at the door of his private office talking to one of the directors as we walked by. He said to my boss, 'Tom, that was a very good presentation you made to the directors this morning. Congratulations.' My boss said, 'Thanks. I'm glad you liked it.'

He gets only grudging recognition

"It happens," Larry said, "that I wrote that presentation. But do you think he would tell me that it went over so well? No, not on your life. As we rode down in the elevator together I said to him, 'Evidently they liked the presentation I wrote for you.' He didn't look too happy about that. He just said, 'Yes, it was all right.'

"Everything I do for him and all the speeches I write for him go over big. You'd think that he would appreciate that enough to get me a raise. His salary is more than four times as much as mine! And I've been trying to get him to approve an increase in my salary for two years and he just keeps putting me off. You see why I need that drink?"

Why no salary increase in two years

I told Larry that I could understand why he would be exasperated. I said, "There must be a reason why he won't have your salary increased. Do you think that he might be afraid that you could take over his job?"

Larry said, "I doubt that. It wouldn't make any difference to him anyway because he's a wealthy man. Of course I can do anything he can do. As I told you, I do most of his work and write all of his speeches. For instance, I have just finished writing a speech that he is going to deliver at a big national convention in San Francisco. He's the principal speaker and I wrote every word of his speech. When he comes back from these conventions, he never tells me how the speech I wrote went over unless I ask him. That's the kind of a fellow he is."

"What do you say to your boss when he comes back from one of those speaking trips?" I asked.

Larry said, "I usually ask, 'Well, how did my speech go over at the convention?'"

Hurting another's feelings can be costly

I asked, "Larry, has it ever occurred to you that perhaps you haven't been able to get what you want because you may have been irritating your boss? He may resent your patting yourself on the back when you talk to him about the things you do for him."

Larry said, "I think I can understand the point you're making. You think I've been blowing my own horn too much with him."

How often do you tell your boss you appreciate something he has done?

"That is part of it," I said. "But let me ask you another question, Larry. How often do you tell him that you like something he has done or that you appreciate something he has done?"

Larry said, "I don't. He doesn't tell me he appreciates anything I've done so why should I tell him that I appreciate anything he's done?"

I asked, "You want an increase in salary, don't you?"

"Yes," Larry said.

"You've been with this company for more than seven years and you like the organization and the people in it, don't you?"

"Yes."

"If I can suggest a way to improve your relationship with your boss and get that increase in salary you want, would you try it?"

"Yes I would," Larry said.

I said, "The convention in San Francisco is an industry-wide convention so probably a number of the other executives of your company will be going out there with your boss. When they all come back, before you say anything to your boss, ask some of the others how Tom's speech was received. Probably they will tell you it went over in a big way. You wrote it and you know it was good.

"This time, however, instead of asking your boss to tell you how your speech went over, tell him that you heard from some of the others who attended the convention that his presentation was a very successful one. Then ask him what he thought of the convention—and listen while he tells you.

"Compliment him on his part in the convention. Ask him if he would like to have you send his speech to the public relations department for release to business papers."

Larry said, "You mean you want me to butter him up?"

Look at this from his point of view

"That isn't what I mean," I said. "You have been telling me how you have wanted words of appreciation from him. Doesn't it occur to you that he also might like to hear an expression of appreciation from you?"

Larry said, "Yes, I suppose you're right."

I reminded him that he had agreed to try the formula for improving his relationship with his boss and getting an increase in salary. I said, "Don't stop showing your appreciation for him after your comments about the San Francisco convention. At least two or three times every week find something that he does that you honestly can appreciate. Then tell him that you appreciate it.

Look for the other person's good qualities

"Every day look for the good things that he is doing. You said he is a charming person and that is true. He must have many good qualities. Look for these. Let him know that you recognize them. Show him that you appreciate him. Show him that you really are interested in him as a person not just as a boss."

I asked Larry to try this formula for several months and then tell me what happened. He said he would.

A few months later he called. He said, "The strained relationship I had with Tom is just about gone. It's much more pleasant to work with him. And, believe it or not, I think I'm going to get the increase in salary I wanted."

He followed Lord Chesterfield's advice and it worked!

What brought about the change in Larry's relationship with his boss? Larry followed a formula based on the advice Lord Chesterfield gave many years ago. Lord Chesterfield said: "Make the other person like himself a little better and I promise you he will like you very well indeed."

When Larry Rogers showed that he recognized some of the good things that his boss did and complimented him for them, he made his boss feel a little better. Consequently, this man, being human, began to like Larry much more than he had before. After Larry had been showing his appreciation of the boss for a few months, this gentleman was willing to listen and listen favorably to Larry's suggestions. He reacted the way Larry wanted him to. Larry got his salary increase.

There is a wrong way and a right way to get what you want

Of course, you might say that the boss is the one who should have given Larry the recognition he deserved. This is true. But we have been discussing Larry's problem in trying to secure a better relationship and more money. He had been communicating the wrong way with the man who could give him the thing he wanted. When he began to follow the ABC techniques of the human side of effective communication, he got the results which he had been unable to get before.

When he learned to sense the boss's needs and reactions, when he communicated with the boss in terms of this man's own interests and showed that he was interested in him, he was able to communicate successfully and achieve the results he wanted.

It pays to show that you are interested in the men and women with whom you work

Remember Lord Chesterfield's advice and you will never forget the very important part three of the ABC technique for successful communications—show your interest in the other person. When you show the other person that you are really interested in him, you make him like himself a little better and he will like you very well indeed.

Some employers do not think it necessary to demonstrate a personal interest in the people who work for them. A sales manager said, "I pay my men enough. Either they produce for me or I get others who can." This manager is thought of as a cold blooded martinet by his salesmen and he has a heavy and costly turnover. He loses many good men who are human enough to want a word of appreciation as well as a respectable salary.

Show that you appreciate them

Human beings are not machines. You don't plug them into an electric socket, press a button, and automatically get the action you want. You get it through their minds. Keep open your contact with the minds of those with whom you work by showing them you appreciate what they do for you.

Compliment someone who does a particularly good job. If your stenographer types letters and reports for you that you are proud to sign, tell her about this. If you supervise salesmen and some of your men sell more than their quotas, send them a note of congratulations. Let them know you appreciate them. If you work in a store or bank or service station, don't take customers for granted. Thank them each time they come in.

Let them know you do appreciate them. This will make them like you very much indeed!

Get into the habit of sending "thank you" notes. Send them to everyone who does you a favor, or gives you an order, or goes out of his way to help you. The men and women with whom you work want to know how they stand with you. Show them you appreciate them.

These men wanted to know where they stood with the boss

The Agency Management Association of Hartford, Connecticut conducted a study among 234 insurance agents who had terminated their employment. The Association asked the former employers to classify the men as desirable agents or as undesirable ones. They were interested particularly in why the "desirable" agent decides to quit his job. They found that more than twice as many desirable agents as undesirable ones said they quit because of such disagreeable aspects of their jobs as "not knowing where I stand with the manager," or "the fact that the manager really isn't interested in me."

They needed psychological security

In interpreting these findings, S. Rains Wallace, Jr., Director of Research for the Association, said, "While we have talked and fretted about economic security, agents have sought (and too often failed to find) *psychological* security—the feeling that the boss was on their side, knowing and sympathizing with their problems, and giving the inspiration which they required as individuals."

Here again is evidence of the fact that human beings need to know that others are interested in them. When you recognize this fact and show your interest in the people with whom you work, you'll find that they are much more interested in listening to you, in understanding you, and reacting the way you want them to.

Too often supervisors communicate with their employees only when it is necessary to discipline the employee. This is unfortunate because many workers place a big chip on their shoulders when they see the boss coming toward them. As one of them said to a man working next to him when he saw his foreman approaching, "What is that big jerk going to try to shove down our throats now?"

Give them a pat on the back—they need it

This is a sad situation but a common one. Too many of us, workers and supervisors, talk to others in terms of our own interests. We want others to show their appreciation for us. It often doesn't occur to us to show our appreciation for them.

If supervisors would only remember that the men and women under them would like to have a pat on the back occasionally, they would find they could communicate much more successfully at all times, even during periods of stress, because the people working for them would *want* to listen to what they had to say.

Workers want to be on good terms with the boss

Lawrence Appley, President of American Management Association, said, "Even though there seems to be evidence to the contrary, I believe the average person likes to know what the boss thinks of his work, likes to have constructive suggestions about how he might do better, and likes to be rewarded when he improves, both by financial and non-financial means. Most people want to be on good terms with the boss and to enjoy his respect and confidence.

"Some time ago I was present at a meeting of a training committee of an organization. The committee was developing a course of instruction for first-line supervisors. The union president was a member of the committee. His contribution was constructive and profound.

Talk to fellow workers about things
they want to talk about

"The union president pointed out that the average worker has personal contact with the foreman only when he has done something wrong and when the foreman comes around to correct or discipline him. He pointed out that this is not a particularly desirable way for a supervisor to be remembered. He argued that foremen should be trained in how to talk with employees when things are going well and how to talk with them about the things employees want to talk about.

"Most people spend a good proportion of their lives with individuals who employ and supervise their efforts. This time could and should be pleasant, regardless of how monotonous, routine, or minor the work may seem to be. If there is any job on the payroll that does not have value, it should not be there. And if it has value, the person doing it should recognize the value and take pride in doing the job well.

Spend more time in individual consultation

"When a friendly, helpful boss is considerate enough and good manager enough to spend some time with his people in individual consultation, these can be considered as nothing else but precious moments. They certainly bear fruit and form fond memories."

The union president suggested that foremen be trained to talk with employees when things are going well and talk with them about the things employees want to talk about. Lawrence Appley said that the time spent in such communication could be considered "as nothing else but precious moments." And he added, "They certainly bear fruit and form fond memories."

Show them you're really interested in them

Why is this true? You know the answer—when you show the people with whom you work that you really are interested in them, you make them like themselves a little better and therefore they like you very well indeed. They are inclined to listen favorably to whatever you have to say.

How do we show others that we are really interested in them? Suppose we review the method suggested in Chapter Three and see how they apply to successful communications on the job: We demonstrate our interest in others (1) through our recognition, (2) through our attention, (3) through the tone of our voice, (4) through our actions, (5) through our appearance.

How recognition demonstrates interest

When anyone approaches you, look up and greet him cheerfully. Call him by name. Show him that you recognize him as an important individual. You know this will make him like himself a little better!

How your attention shows your interest

When another person speaks to you, concentrate your attention on him. Look him in the eye. One of the most successful supervisors said he could tell you the color of the eyes of every person with whom he worked. Do you know the color of the eyes of the last two or three people with whom you have talked? When you give others your complete attention, they are much more inclined to give you theirs.

How the tone of your voice reveals your interest

Does your voice sound friendly? It should. Macy's, the big New York department store, had mirrors placed in front of each person in the telephone order department. When one of these people looked into the mirror and saw a frown, he didn't like it, so he smiled. The smile was reflected in his voice and Macy's telephone sales took a sharp upward increase. Put a smile in your voice when you talk to others with whom you work and you will be happy with the sound you hear in their voices when they speak to you.

How your actions indicate your interest

When you see you can help someone do something, help him. Go out of your way to cooperate with the others with whom you work. Your actions will tell them that you are interested in them and they will be much more interested in anything that you have to say.

How your appearance reflects your interest

A sales manager told me that he felt one of his men could be the most successful one on the sales force if he would only become more interested in his appearance. He would wear the same shirt for two or three days. His trousers were baggy. His shoes unshined. This man happened to be a college graduate but he said he just never had paid much attention to the way he looked. When he heard that customers called his office and complained that his sloppy appearance suggested he wasn't interested in getting any of their business, he agreed that perhaps this could affect his success. When he improved his appearance he made a better impression on people and they were more inclined to listen to what he had to say.

When I was discussing this third part of the ABC communication technique—show the other person that you are interested in him—with a business executive, he said, "You're telling people to be obsequious. You're recommending self-abasement."

You can be forceful if you show you really are interested in the success of those with whom you work

I assured him I was recommending no such thing. I told him about the first talk a friend of mine had with his salesmen. He is general sales manager of one division of a large organization. He told his several hundred salesmen, "I didn't take this job to win a popularity contest. I don't want to be the best liked sales manager in the United States. I want to be the manager of the most successful salesmen in this country. I have one interest, and one interest only, and that is in helping each of you become more successful. I am going to devote all my time and energy to this purpose." This certainly is not obsequiousness or self-abasement. However, it is a good example of talking to others in terms of their interest—success—and showing your interest in them by helping them become more successful.

Five years later my friend was still showing his men that he was interested in helping each one of them become more successful. They respect him and work hard for him. When he was appointed sales manager, his division was losing more than five million dollars a year. At the end of five years, it was earning a net profit of more than ten million dollars a year. Evidently it does help to show the people with whom you work that you are interested in them.

Make those around you at work like themselves a little better—and they'll help you become more successful

To communicate more successfully at work, remember the ABC of effective communication on the human side: (A) Study the other person, learn to sense his needs and his reactions, so you can (B) communicate with him in terms of his own interests. And be sure to (C) show him that you're interested in him!

Never neglect the third part of this ABC technique. As Lord Chesterfield said, "Make the other person like himself a little better and I promise you that he will like you very well indeed."

*"It is only with the heart that one can see rightly;
what is essential is invisible to the eye."*

ANTOINE DE SAINT-EXUPÉRY

Conclusion

THE KEY TO SUCCESSFUL HUMAN RELATIONS

The union president who suggested to the members of a training committee that foremen should be trained to talk with employees when things are going well, and how to talk with them about the things employees want to talk about, gave that committee the key to successful human relations—*show the other person that you really are interested in him.*

And this is the key to successful human relations at home as well as at work. If a husband and wife learn to talk with each other when things are going well and if each talks about the things the other wants to talk about, they will have an understanding and an appreciation of each other that will carry them through the periods of stress every family is sure to have.

People resent evidence of indifference

The union president indicated that foremen's difficulties with their men may be due to the fact that they seldom talk with them until it is necessary to correct or discipline them.

Why this lack of friendly contact? Probably because some supervisors think the men are paid to do the work and it isn't necessary to show a personal interest in them.

Successful communication gets better results
than money or other incentives

This is a serious mistake. Money, or incentives, will buy passive cooperation. The threat of force may produce antagonistic cooperation. But successful communication, especially when this is carried on over a period of time, produces enthusiastic voluntary cooperation—at home or at work.

We learn much about ourselves by observing the reactions of animals. During the five years George F. Morse was Director of the Boston Zoological Park he made a close study of the many animals in his charge. He said, "We study the psychology of animals, discover their reactions to all sorts of conditions and try to give them the conditions that suit them best. We know that a happy, contented animal is usually a healthy one. To that end we try to make all our animals happy and contented.

He tries to understand them

"Wherever I am in charge of animals I try to visit every one of them once a day and talk and play with them. Do not think by that remark that I am boasting of my ability to speak monkey language and the language of other animals fluently. I am not able to do that, but we who are in continual charge of these animals get to recognize certain sounds which they make as meaning something. They have a language among themselves. They have sounds which mean anticipation, pleasure, jealousy, hatred, hunger, and many other things.

"Each morning when I go into my lion house I stick my head in the door and make an imitation sound to which the lions roar with anticipation and pleasure. When the lions hear that sound they wake up, stretch themselves, and make an answering roar at me just the same as if to say: 'Why, good morning. Come in. We are glad to see you.' I come in. I go inside the guard rail. The big beasts rub themselves up against the bars. I pull the ear of one; scratch the neck of another; tickle another's ribs. They like it because it varies the monotony of their day, and they have something to look forward to.

"When I took charge of the Boston Zoo I found the lions, tigers, and leopards kept in an old ramshackle building. There was no sanitation, no sunlight, no fresh air in those cages. I worked pretty hard on the City Council before I got an appropriation to build a new house. Finally I got it. I built a lion house with outside cages and earthen floors, and inside cages twice as big as the old ones. There was sunlight in this house and fresh air. It was such a lion house that if I was a lion I would be tickled to death to live in it.

"Moving day was going to be an exciting one. You never know what is going to happen when you are moving a bunch of powerful animals. Ropes break, keepers get hurt, animals get hurt.

They were to be offered an "incentive" to cooperate

"All of the animals had gone hungry for 48 hours so that we could bait them with a piece of raw meat into a shifting box, eight or nine feet long, by three feet wide and four feet high. It is made out of two-inch oak planks. At one end there is a trap door which we put up against the door of the animal's cage. At the other end there is a little barred door through which we can look to see when the animal comes into the box so as to know when to release the trap door.

"Jim was a big fine male lion and he was going to have the honor of being the first one to occupy the new house. Now, there is an interesting story in regard to Jim. We used to have games together very often when I would come to the lion house. I would turn on the lights. He would see me coming. I would crouch down behind a little post about four inches square and sneak up behind it pretending that I was hiding myself. He would do the same thing behind a little post in his cage. These posts did not hide us at all. When we would get behind these posts we would wait there for a minute for the other to move. Jim was always the best waiter. I had to move first. I would come from behind the post, rush in on him, striking and growling as wildly as I could. Jim would come rushing at me striking and growling, and I would jump away from him. We would dance back and forth that way for five or six minutes, and it would always wind up the same way. When Jim got tired of playing he would come down in front, rub up against the bars, and I would pet him.

"Well, Jim was going to have the honor of being the first lion in the new house. He did not like the looks of the box. There was something about that box that reminded him perhaps of some former time when he got his tail caught in a trap door. He sulked back into the corner of his cage and lay there snarling.

Jim could not be bribed

"They showed him the raw meat and even though he had nothing to eat for two days he would not look at it. They dangled it in front of his eyes but he could not be budged.

"They took iron rods and tried to pry him out of his corner. He just bit at them until I was afraid he would break his teeth.

"They turned the hose on him. You know how a cat hates water, but he just snarled and growled at the water.

"After working about 30 minutes to no avail the head keeper came back and said: 'Mr. Morse, I am afraid we have got to rope him.' I said, 'We can't do that. Something might happen to him like that lion in the Philadelphia Zoo. He may break his leg or injure himself. He is the finest animal in captivity and one of the best lions I have got. I am afraid to have anything like that happen to him.'

"He said, 'What can we do?' I thought for a moment and said, 'I have got an idea.' He looked at me in astonishment and said, 'I have done everything.' I said, 'Get all the men outside.' He did that.

Jim recognized the voice of a friend

"When it was all quiet in the lion house I started walking slowly towards Jim's cage and I talked to him in the same tone of voice I used when talking to other animals I care for. Jim didn't understand any word I spoke but he did understand by my expression and tone of voice that I was a friend to him.

"When I got half-way to his cage I gave that roar of pleasure that he and I used to give each other every morning at nine o'clock when I came to see him. Jim got to his feet, looked around, did not see anybody but me and made an answering roar.

"He came right up to the bars and rubbed his head and mane against the bars wanting me to pet him, which I did.

"Finally I said, 'Come on Jimmy, let us go for a little walk.' And I walked towards the shifting box. He kept company with me inside his cage. When we got to the shifting box I said, 'Come on, Jimmy, come on, old fellow, come right into this box.' Without hesitation that big creature walked right into the box."

Successful communication gets the cooperation
which incentives and force could not produce

They couldn't induce this lion to cooperate with them by offering him the "incentive" of big chunks of raw meat. He wouldn't budge, even though he had been starved for 48 hours and was ravenously hungry. They couldn't get his cooperation by force. But when someone who had been communicating respect, understanding, and appreciation to him for many months came in, that big, powerful lion walked by his side like a contented puppy.

This experience indicates that everything we do and say to others today, tomorrow, and every day can affect our ability to communicate with them successfully at some future time, especially during periods of stress.

*Build a backlog of confidence and you'll have
much more influence over others*

In our daily contacts with others at home and at work we
are building up a backlog of confidence or of indifference.

We may not realize this until some critical moment when we
need their cooperation or understanding.

This story also emphasizes a factor which influences our
success in "getting through" to another person which often is
more powerful than any words we could possibly use. I call
this "the radar of human relations."

In my book, *The Human Side of Selling,** I said, "We have

a receiving apparatus that is more powerful, more sensitive and
more far reaching than our ears, our eyes or any of our senses.
This receiving apparatus—this 'radar of human relations'—is
the heart. When you meet another person, his heart tunes you
in. It picks up your wave length, and he listens intently. He
listens for the answer to the biggest question in human relations: *'Is he with me or against me?'*

"The other person 'feels' the answer. And if he feels that you
are interested only in making him do what you want him to
do, that you have no interest in him personally, then he knows
that you are against him—and whatever you do or say will make
little impression on him."

*We resist those who show they are indifferent to us,
but we cooperate with those who are our friends*

When the men in the Boston Zoological Park tried to get that
big lion to cooperate with them, they offered to "pay" him with
the food he needed, and he was starving. But he refused to
move. When they tried force, he just growled at them.

However, when George Morse appeared, that lion's "radar"
told him, "Here is my friend, the one who is really interested in
me!" And you know what happened—even though he could

---

* Published by Harper & Brothers, New York.

not understand Mr. Morse's words, he got the message. He listened. He understood. He reacted the way his friend wanted him to.

In his magnificent book, *The Little Prince*,* Antoine de Saint-Exupéry said, "Men have no more time to understand anything. They buy things already made at the shops. But there is no shop anywhere where one can buy friendship, and so men have no friends any more." And he gave this secret we must remember if we want to make friends: *"It is only with the heart that one can see rightly; what is essential is invisible to the eye."*

When those with whom you live and work tune you in, and listen for the answer to the key question in human relations: "Are you with me or against me?" see that you are answering sincerely, "I am with you, friend, all the way!"

The key to successful human relations

This is the key essential in human relations—show others that you are interested in them, in their point of view, in everything about them.

Study them so you can learn to sense their needs and their reactions (remember how George Morse studied the animals with whom he worked to learn their needs and their reactions? It's much more important for you to study the human beings with whom you live and work so you can learn to understand them). Communicate with them in terms of their own interests, and in every way you can, show your interest in them.

When you use this ABC technique, your communications will be successful. Those with whom you live and work will *want* to listen to you, understand you and react the way you want them to. You will have the key to successful human relations.

Index

189

ABOUT THE AUTHOR

Teacher, lecturer, advertising executive, former President of the Moore Institute of Chicago, Robert E. Moore has been a close student of communication techniques. He is also author of *Turn on the Green Lights in Your Life, The Human Side of Selling,* and *Automation in Business Communication.*